JOAN PARRY DUTTON

The Flower World of Williamsburg

Color Photography by FRANK J. DAVIS

THE COLONIAL WILLIAMSBURG FOUNDATION
Williamsburg, Virginia

Distributed by Holt, Rinehart and Winston
New York, New York

Library of Congress Catalog Card Number 62-18751

Colonial Williamsburg ISBN   0-87935-006-7 (trade)
    0-87935-007-5 (trade paper)

Holt, Rinehart and Winston ISBN   0-03-007686-2

REVISED EDITION, 1973

Second printing, 1976

Printed in the United States of America

Contents

List of Illustrations

The Flower World of Williamsburg

Why This Book

ONE spring and summer, then a newcomer from my native England and outward bound on a three-year spree to see America by way of its gardens, I lived in a house on Duke of Gloucester Street.

"Doesn't Colonial Williamsburg remind you very much of England?" people asked me time and time again.

"No," I used to reply those first few weeks, "really, it doesn't at all. I think it is itself, wholly eighteenth-century Virginia." So I judged it, by the history books. But my answer, I could tell, was invariably a trifle disappointing, although to my mind perfect eighteenth-century Virginia seemed as proud a distinction as any citizen could want.

Naturally, at first not only Williamsburg but Virginia too was new to me, and to the exclusion of much else I noted the differences in commonplace things. The white wood-frame houses and white picket fences did not belong to any English scene I knew. The fringe tree that I watched day by day as the white flower clusters opened and then hung down with their weight of bloom, the dogwoods, and the paper mulberries with their queer contorted trunks—all were unfamiliar. Boxwood and elm trees are English as can be, but the upsoaring elms on the William and Mary campus and around Bruton Parish Church were different from English elms.

And I had never seen box, a feature of so many Virginia gardens, grow in such billowing abundance. Nor had I imagined that the Southern magnolia, which I knew as a prized exotic trained up the side of an English south-facing wall, could grow to the stature of the three towering trees I saw and marveled at from my bedroom window.

Sounds were different. The slow drawl of Southern speech was as noticeable to me as my English accent was to my neighbors. And the mockingbird, whose song compares in beauty to that of the English nightingale, called a different tune.

As the weeks wore on, however, and first impressions gave way to a sense of familiarity, of feeling at home, I began to notice that Colonial Williamsburg did, after all, have a very English air. One day the truth dawned on me. The Englishness of Williamsburg was not of my own time, nor was it so intended; it was of the England of two centuries and more ago. If at first I was a little startled that "old" Williamsburg looked so new—my preconception of the town had led me to expect buildings mellowed by time and weather—I reflected that to the colonists it *was* new and new looking, and I was seeing it very much as they had.

The Great Union flag that flies from the cupola of the Capitol from sunrise to sunset every day—and which pulled my glance upward each morning as I left the house nearby—was, I discovered, different only in small detail from the Union Jack I knew. While Williamsburg is the only place in the United States, except the English consulates and the embassy in Washington, daily to fly a British flag, it is the only place in the world to fly the Great Union flag of Queen Anne's reign: the banner carried by red-coated British soldiers in the Revolutionary War.

When the time came for me to start on my garden sight-seeing adventure over America, I resolved to return one day to Williamsburg. It was the flag, I think, and the fact that here was one of the great crossroads in the history of gardening, that sparked my wish to trace the association of Williamsburg with the mother country through gardens and flowers, as architects and interior designers have done through buildings and their furnishings. Above all, I wanted to trace that association through the use of flowers *in the home*.

Arboretums contain great collections of rare and beautiful plants, and often fine libraries. Famous showplace gardens, designed to fit contemporary fashion and meet laborsaving demands, may have more dramatic appeal than, say, the formal garden of the Governor's Palace. And America's great flower shows may, as such, rival the best anywhere in the world. But in the broad view, the flower world of Colonial Williamsburg is unique.

The reconstructed gardens give a forceful impression of colonial garden art, modeled after that of England, but unmatched in England today because the old gardens there have undergone constant changes of fashion to suit the tastes of successive owners and periods. More-over, Colonial Williamsburg maintains daily, the year around, an ever fresh and changing display of flowers in its exhibition buildings. It is a highly exclusive display in the sense that the flowers and containers are only those that were known and loved and used by housewives—and queens—of the eighteenth century.

When my grand tour was at an end, and I looked back over the long miles of travel and the acres of gardens I had seen, my thoughts again turned to Williamsburg and to its bouquets of flowers. The months had stretched into years; I had become an American, and a Californian. But my resolution stuck. I did go back to old Williamsburg, a journey that was to prove longer in time than in miles, more a reliving of history than of merely rewalking Williamsburg streets.

This is the story of that journey.

I looked, as at the reflection in a mirror, into the eighteenth-century English garden in its heyday, and into Virginia plantation life in its youth of romance and great names. I followed both the hazardous explorings of English plantsmen who gathered the as yet unknown flowers of the Virginia wilderness and the triumphs and disappoint-ments of those devoted English and Virginia gardeners who essayed to grow the wild discoveries in their gardens.

Then I took another look, a reeducated look, at what I can only describe—by its adherence to the ways and means available to the early Virginia housewife—as the way flowers were used for decoration in the home in colonial days.

By such roundabout journeying I came at last to understand the why and wherefore of the flowers that now brighten the rooms and add welcoming warmth to the houses in the Historic Area. I must also acknowledge the efforts of Edna Pennell—now retired, she was Colo-nial Williamsburg's flower supervisor—who did the arrangements pic-tured on these pages.

An Acknowledgment

Acknowledgments usually include the names of those to whom a writer is indebted. Here I use the word acknowledgment in the collec-tive singular. A list of the people who have helped me to make this book would read like the telephone directory of a small country town. For there are some who have spent time and thought on the text and its illustrations, and there are many others, friends as well as associates, who, perhaps in unsuspected ways, have helped me to know and love Williamsburg past and present. The two small words *Thank You* in no way adequately express my appreciation.

The Flower World of Williamsburg

I

Gardening's Greatest Era

TO MAKE MEN LOVE their country, one must make their country lovely. So summed up the eighteenth-century statesman Edmund Burke, friend of America in the British Parliament when Virginia was a colony that reached boundlessly westward —and Williamsburg was still young.

In our own day of whirling wheels, billboards, tin cans, and international alarums it takes effort to wrench one's thoughts from the world-that-is to Burke's world-that-was and to conceive of a statesman's hailing beauty as strength. Edmund Burke, however, sounded no lone trumpet. In England and Virginia alike, he spoke in harmony with the time.

It was a time that, for English-speaking people, historians have called both the Age of Reason and the Age of Taste. I, garden-loving, like to think of it as the Age of Flowers. In America, colonial houses and gardens, built English-style, added a touch of the then "back home" to the newly cultivated countryside. In the air was the wine of discovery of the wonders of a boundless

◀ 2. Boxwood parterres and a touch of the topiary that so charmed King William.

1

opening the door to a wondrously new floral treasury in the Virginia wilderness.

By the time Francis Bacon, England's finest intellect and a garden lover as well, printed his essay, *Of Gardens*, in 1625, he could describe enough "Things of Beautie . . . for all the Moneths in the Yeare." His emphasis was on fragrant herbs and flowers. And certainly Bacon foresaw how his flower list would grow. His essay envisioned the garden of a century thence, not, as many now think, a contemporary English garden.

John Parkinson, the royal apothecary of Charles I, followed Bacon by publishing, in 1629, Britain's first great garden book, *Paradisi in sole Paradisus Terrestris*. Translated as Parkinson's *Park-in-Sun*— "Paradise" being used in the old sense of the word: an enclosed pleasure garden or park—the Latin title was more than a pun on the author's name. Parkinson was able to list a growing array of foreign or "outlandish" flowers, called by an earlier writer "exoticks." Too, he reported the rise of the florist and nurseryman whose skill in hybridizing was adding to the sizes and colors of blooms. He listed nearly 150 varieties of tulips alone that were now "feathered" or "striped" or "made bizarre" by the new art.

Especially of interest is that *Paradisi* described a wholly new kind of garden, one within the range and pocketbook of the ordinary householder. At last, the small home garden was about to have a place among its royal and noble neighbors.

Many Virginia flowers are mentioned in *Paradisi*. Most of them had been introduced by John Tradescant, whom botanists know as Tradescant the Elder. He had an interest in the Virginia Company, the first landlord of the colony, and although he never set foot on Virginia soil, he was an eager recipient from "noblemen, gentlemen, and sea commaunders" of "such toyes as they could bring from other parts." Tradescant the Elder scoured Europe for "exoticks" and explored for new plants in Russia and Algeria. He was the first of a long line of British plant collectors who were to splash floral color across England's countryside.

Then, an epochal event. In 1662, the Royal Society of London was founded to promote all branches of science, with emphasis on natural history. Francis Bacon, although he had died many years earlier, still provided its chief originating influence. In his *New Atlantis* he had described a prophetic scheme of the Royal Society and had urged the

◀ 3. A garden, walks, and a tree-framed vista reveal the "pleasures of planting."

writing of a complete natural history "to restore to humanity its lost dominion over the material world."

He had foreseen that so vast a work would require the help and money of royal, noble, and wealthy benefactors. As at no other time in no other nation, help and money now rallied to the new call. The Royal Society burgeoned into an exclusive club whose primary aim was the advancement of scientific knowledge. Membership embraced the best names in Britain, but exclusiveness did not rest merely on birth and fortune; talent and ability were as carefully weighed.

Flowers, plants, trees, all growing green things—I doubt if ever they were so much in the forefront of able men's minds as when the seventeenth century turned into the eighteenth, not only in England but wherever able Britishers gathered, and certainly in Virginia. There, the names of those Royal Society notables concerned with the miracles of Nature in new lands overseas were household words.

Among them was Henry Compton, bishop of London, who spoke most eloquently for the clergy. A powerful influence in the court of William and Mary (and incidentally the queen's tutor), he helped secure the charter of the College of William and Mary in Williamsburg and became not only its first chancellor but its adviser, patron, and supporter. No one in England was a better friend of the College's first president, James Blair, and certainly none was a more enthusiastic experimenter with plants. Bishop Compton's garden at Fulham Palace was renowned and had much to do with *flora virginica.*

No less a champion was Sir John Evelyn, Gentleman. His book, *Sylva,* prompted the planting of trees in and around gardens at a time when new glass factories and iron furnaces, hungry for wood fuel, were depleting England of its woodlands. Too, Evelyn saw flowers becoming the motif in all manner of furnishings—a trend that he set down as chapter headings for a book he was too occupied to write. Among many things to be ornamented by floral designs, he listed silk, calico, wallpaper, glassware, wood inlays, and carvings. He is credited with the discovery of Grinling Gibbons, whose superb wood carvings inspired the decoration we see on the newel posts in the Governor's Palace in Williamsburg.

Peter Collinson, as the foremost connoisseur of America's inflowing flowers and plants, represented the rich merchants. We shall get to know him further as our story unfolds. Of the Royal Society's elite, Sir Hans Sloane was outstanding. A great patron of botanists and explorers, his name is remembered in Sloane Street, London, and known to every student of old Williamsburg.

Sir Hans Sloane served as president of both the Royal Society and the College of Physicians. He typified the Old World naturalists: men who lived in the open air and for whom the variety in Nature, as they saw it for the first time, was a constant source of wonderment. All Nature, not gardens alone, was their province. Yet I believe they found more joy in life, following wherever their curiosity led them, than do those specialists of today who concern themselves less with the mystery of the whole than with the activity of a single plant genus.

Sir Hans was a happy man whose life may be summed up by a description of Sloane Street. It is "very long, obviously prosperous, and perfectly straight." From it, in his day, he could walk in minutes into open fields and tree-lined lanes and smell the flowers and the freshly turned earth.

An avid collector of Nature's "curiosities," manuscripts, and books, he left his vast collections to the nation. They formed the nucleus of the British Museum, opened by George II. One need not visit the Museum, however, to see the fullest expression of Sir Hans Sloane's work. He was the unfailing friend of botanists, plant collectors, hybridizers, gardeners with original ideas, in short of all those pioneers who were laying the foundations of the gardens we enjoy today. It took new knowledge and careful experience to make the exotics from abroad adaptable to the English climate and to make the beloved old English flowers and shrubs adaptable to the climates of the New World. Sir Hans Sloane and his colleagues of the Royal Society—but above all Sloane—made it possible to assemble that knowledge.

William and Mary were Sir Hans's colleagues in the very best sense of that term. They stand unique in Britain's history as the only sovereigns ever to have been jointly proclaimed king and queen, he as the Dutch prince, William of Orange, Mary as a princess of the House of Stuart. So, jointly too, they refurbished the gardens of Hampton Court, William concerning himself with design, Mary with her flowers; the two loved the gardens as no other king or queen before or since. Indirectly, through the additions they made at Hampton Court, they influenced what were to be the gardens of colonial Williamsburg.

William, who had acquired a taste for the French style, ordered the great fountain garden, a semicircular parterre, to be set against Sir Christopher Wren's new east front of the Palace. And, faithful to Dutch tradition, he brought to a climax the art of topiary—greens trained and clipped into strange, startling shapes. He added a maze and had Sir Christopher design an entire topiary fort complete with bastions, battlements, escarpments, and artillery.

As gates for the Great Fountain Garden he ordered panels of wrought-iron screens. *Treillage* or trellis work became more elaborate. Leaden figures of boys bearing baskets were set atop the Flower Pot Gate, again designed by Wren. Daniel Marot, a Huguenot refugee from Holland, was commissioned to make garden vases and the fashionable delftware. Figures and "urnes" and "vauzes" were scattered throughout the gardens.

Meanwhile, Queen Mary indulged her fondness for rare plants. Her tutor, Bishop Compton, may have been the first to kindle her interest in them, and from William she would know that exotics had been grown in the Netherlands earlier than anywhere else. "Tulipomania," the craze for tulips that caused Hollanders to gamble in rare bulbs as in stocks and bonds, had come and gone fifty years before. Nonetheless, that strange episode of garden history must still have been in William's mind and may account for Mary self-consciously excusing the cost of keeping her "exoticks" in hothouses heated by flues and furnaces and for sending to Virginia one of the Hampton Court gardeners, James Road, to make a collection of "foreigne Plantes." She knew her hobby "drew an expense after it," but, as she apologized, it was her only extravagance, and as it was one that "employed many hands, she hoped it would be forgiven her."

It must be acknowledged that William and Mary were fortunate in having in their service two notable gardeners, George London and Henry Wise. The two men were friends and partners in the famous Brompton Park Nurseries, which they founded. Between them they directed most of the great gardens in England. London, at one time gardener to Bishop Compton, was appointed Royal Gardener (and a Page of the Backstairs to the Queen); Wise later became Royal Gardener to Queen Anne.

Daniel Defoe, best known for his *Robinson Crusoe* and one of the outstanding figures of the early English novel and journalism, summed up the influence of William and Mary on English life by crediting each with the introduction of two customs: the queen, the love of fine East India calicoes and of furnishing houses with ceramics; the king, with lending royal prestige to the love of both gardening and painting. Defoe noticed that "all the gentlemen of England began to fall in" with the king's taste for gardening, "and in a few years fine gardens and fine houses began to grow up in every corner . . . the gentlemen

4. *Treillage* or trellis work became more elaborate.

followed everywhere with such gust that the alteration is indeed wonderful through the whole kingdom."

Apart from the country gentlemen's seats, he went on, the countryside was "bespangled with villages; those villages filled with houses, and the houses surrounded with gardens, walks, vistas, avenues, representing all the beauties of building, and all the pleasures of planting."

The yeoman, "he who cultivates the ground and is independent," was a free man with full right to vie with his king, which he did in a manner that must have made Dutch William feel more at home in England. The yeoman's counterpart in Holland was the small landholder whose garden of modest size was divided into small sections by hedges or canals. It was just the kind of garden best suited and most appealing to the yeoman and his cottage.

Leonard Meager's book, *The English Gardener*, reflected the trend. A homely, sound, and simple work, it went through eleven editions by 1710. Philip Miller, distinguished gardener, wrote in 1722 of the "considerable pitch" to which gardening had arrived during the thirty years just past.

British trade was increasing, prosperity was mounting apace, and the lesser gentry had the means more readily to follow the great. Yeoman and cottager could now march with the gentry. Up and down and all across the country, there were gardens everywhere.

While Queen Mary reveled in her exotics, William reveled in greens. Their reign, and also that of Queen Anne who succeeded them to the throne, was associated with the cultivation of greens of every kind—although Anne ordered all the box removed from the royal gardens because she disliked the scent. Topiary work had long been practiced in England, but the Dutch were the acknowledged masters of this art of green sculpture and William adored it. With the king leading by example, the green craze now boomed—above all for greens of bright, shining foliage, and topiary work. To such fantastic extremes was topiary carried that writers flourished derisive pens at the absurdity of gardens peopled by such strange beasts and birds. Wrote Joseph Addison in *The Spectator*, "Our trees rise in cones, globes and pyramids. We see the marks of scissors upon every plant and bush . . . for my own part, I would rather look upon a tree in all its luxuriancy, then when it is thus cut and trimmed into a mathematical figure."

Ridicule proved to be the baptismal blessing of a new profession. The pursuit of natural history, the curiosities coming in from overseas, made Englishmen view the world as startingly new. They became aware, as never before, of the beauty of their own countryside. It was time for change. The gentry of Queen Anne's day were ready to go along with the rising school of professional garden designers—landscape gardeners or architects we call them today—who believed that a garden should blend with, and not be hedged off from, the landscape. The paradox is that William, who loved formality, carried it to the point of what amounted to its suicide. Its critics, fortified by the writers' jibes, were soon able to broomsweep topiary and most other formal garden embellishments out of their path as they rushed headlong to merge garden into park and park into landscape.

The surfeit of formality, however, was only one of the currents mak-

5. This Chinese Chippendale style fence fronting the Lightfoot House suggests the influence of chinoiserie.

ing for change. England was just entering her great era of lawnmaking. The lawnmower was still far in the future, but observing gardeners could not help note that England's climate favored grass, whole broad cropped expanses of green velvet. And there were men who knew how to make hand-swung scythes shear as evenly as any machine-to-be.

Another undercurrent was trade—especially the trade with China and the Dutch that brought to England fragile porcelains, lustrous silks, and painted wallpapers. *Chinoiserie*, having gained a foothold on English taste during the reign of Charles II, became a cult. The porcelain tower of Nanking was declared to be the eighth wonder of the world. So-called Chinese wallpaper, Chippendale's new chairs, and Dutch delftware reflected impressions of oriental art and provided a welcome and reasonable breakaway from stiff formality and convention. The curve was rediscovered to be softer than the straight line. By such curving lines, by artificial undulations on level ground, by water in pools of irregular shape, *chinoiserie* flowed out from the house into the garden. Even the gazebo, or garden house, which country gentlemen delighted to erect, gave place to the Chinese pagoda.

Yet, for all the revolutionary changes in English gardening, Mary's love for flowers was to outlive William's topiary and all other cults, because it struck home in the common heart. If gardeners of the landscape school were too occupied with design to be concerned with new plants, their numbers were decreasing. Experimental plantsmen, in fact, soon far outnumbered the designers. In the long run, it was they who had an even more lasting effect on the English garden world.

Market gardeners or truck gardeners were growing many more vegetables and learning with the aid of bell glasses—"bee-hives of glass, very curious"—to produce them out of season. The American scarlet (runner) bean, first grown by Tradescant as an ornamental climber, became a standby vegetable ranking with peas and potatoes. Countless new plants—above all from Virginia—were brought in by traders and plant explorers, and the eighteenth century became a passionately flower-minded age. Landscaping was all very well, but for most people, even as with Mary, a garden was no garden at all without flowers.

The coming of the flowers touched the lives and pockets of almost every family in the land, as searchingly but far more happily than taxes do today. They provided explorers with a quickened incentive to search for the fabulous and rare, and even traders of great enterprise lent a hand, trafficking in plants as well as merchandise. Artists were as eager to paint flowers as faces. Pottery was designed specifically for the display of flowers as indoor decoration; textiles and embroideries followed the floral theme. Gardening, in all its branches, stretched long green fingers into a multitude of trades and, in hand with science, profoundly occupied Englishmen's thinking.

Science opened many doors. New methods of engraving increased the artist's and the printer's ranges. Carolus Linnaeus, a Swede, evolved a system of classification of plants. His *Species Plantarum*, published at Stockholm in 1753, has been internationally accepted as the starting point for botanical nomenclature in general.

Down Sloane's long street from Knightsbridge, past what are now Sloane Gardens, and Sloane Square, on toward the River Thames by the King's Road—in Sir Hans's time with nurseymen's gardens stretching far and wide on every hand—as many scientists, artists, plant collectors, and plain dirt gardeners went to visit Philip Miller, curator of

6. "Bee-hives of glass, very curious." Bell glasses were used in the Palace and other Williamsburg gardens.

the Apothecaries' Physic Garden at Chelsea, as went to visit the great Sloane himself.

The Apothecaries' Company had established the physic garden in 1673. (The word "physic" was then used in the sense of pertaining to the physical, that is to natural science, and by no means concerned only drugs. Thus, the Chelsea Physic Garden was in the full sense a botanical garden.) Excursions to see wild plants growing in their natural surroundings were part of the Apothecaries' apprenticeship. Five times a year, the Demonstrator, as the instructor was called, led a party to tramp the fields of outlying London, past Chelsea village to such places as Battersea, where the fritillaries grew as I've seen them still growing in the water meadows near Oxford. The apprentices were allowed to carry neither great coat nor umbrella, but each had a collector's tin box slung over his shoulders. At day's end, awaiting their first full meal of the day at a chosen inn, they opened the boxes and laid out and identified the plants. Generations of English children, I for one, have been brought up in the same plant finding tradition.

The Apothecaries, constantly short of cash, were never able to make their garden fully effective until Sir Hans Sloane bought the Manor of Chelsea in 1722 and leased the garden to them for a nominal five pounds a year. Gardener, not apothecary, Philip Miller became the curator. Philip Miller has had no rival. Rated by his contemporaries as an extremely able botanist and horticulturist, he was skilled especially in acclimatizing exotics from distant parts of widely varied climates. He spoke Latin, as every learned man then did in Europe whatever his nationality, and took an active part in the European traffic of plant exchange.

Philip Miller's personal fame rests today on his introduction of cotton into North America and on his great work, *The Gardener's and Florist's Dictionary*, which was dedicated to the Apothecaries and actually appeared first in 1724. This edition contained the "Catalogue of Ever Greens," twelve in all, including arbutus, bay, box, holly, juniper, laurel, pyracantha, yew, and green privet, which is not properly an evergreen. Seven years later he published *The Gardeners Dictionary* in folio, and it is this that is commonly regarded as the famous work's first edition. Dedicated anew to Sir Hans Sloane, president, and to the Council and Fellows of the Royal Society, it went into eight editions, the last published in 1768. Allowed by "even his enemies to be a work of extraordinary merit," it was the standard authority on gardening for generations of country gentlemen. Thomas Jefferson included it as a "must" for a gentleman's library.

Miller was also a member of the Society of Gardeners, under whose influence floriculture made tremendous advances. Thomas Fairchild, Robert Furber, and Philip Miller, in that order, headed the list of members. They met monthly in a Chelsea coffeehouse to discuss, register, and describe plants growing in their respective gardens and published a *Catalogue* of more than one hundred and fifty trees and shrubs.

Fairchild, a nurseryman, was the first to be concerned with the city gardener and in 1722 published his book by that name. He was also the first to raise and distribute the tulip tree (and probably the catalpa) in quantity, and to this day the bishop of London annually appoints a rector to deliver the Fairchild Lecture in St. Leonard's Shoreditch "On the Wonderful Works of God in the Creation . . ."

Robert Furber, third of the trio, was among the first nurserymen to bring out a catalogue. It went by the elegant name of *Twelve Months of Flowers* and was not profaned by any mention of prices. Its twelve plates, each showing the flowers of the month, were hand-colored en-

7. Furber's bouquet of flowers for November is composed predominantly of Old World plants, but it contains several New World plants, including Virginia Aster, Carolina Star-flower, American Viburnum, French Marigold, Double Nasturtium, Perennial Dwarf Sunflower, and Groundsel Tree.

gravings after the Flemish artist Pieter Casteels and may be seen today, in reproduction, decorating many a house wall in Williamsburg and elsewhere. The catalogue's second edition, *The Flower-Garden Display'd*, appeared in 1732 with text in which Furber pointed out its usefulness, "Not only for the *Curious* in Gardening, but the *Prints* likewise for *Painters, Carvers, Japaners, &c.*, also for the *Ladies*, as Patterns for Working, and Painting in Water-Colours; or Furniture for the Closet."

After Philip Miller's death in 1771 the fame of the Chelsea Physic Garden, although not the interest in its purpose, declined. That interest, growing, led the mother of King George III to establish in 1760 a nine-acre botanical garden that was to become one of the world's foremost: London's Kew Gardens. By 1787, enough people were interested in better gardens to guarantee the success of a radical departure in publishing, the founding of *The Botanical Magazine*, devoted wholly to scientific horticulture and still published.

In 1801, John, the youngest son of Josiah Wedgwood the potter, conceived the idea of forming a society for the improvement of horticulture. Four years later the Horticultural Society of London (now the Royal Horticultural Society) came into being. It was the capstone of the gardening century just closed.

How great was that century may be measured in terms of new flowers, plants, and trees that were added to the English countryside once so predominantly green. When the century began under William (Mary, only thirty-two, had died in 1694 of smallpox) the most optimistic census of "exoticks" in gardens would have counted no more than one thousand. Well before it closed, according to the three-volume *Catalogue of the Plants* being cultivated at Kew Gardens in 1789, the grand total of exotics was five thousand.

How prominently North American plants figured in that increase, we shall see. To the English flower lover, I doubt if any place in North American meant so much as Virginia. The very name stirred the imagination, doubly so, of gardeners who thrilled to the exploits of Mark Catesby. England received many "Things of Beautie" from Catesby, including the greatest book of the day on the natural history of British North American before the Revolution. Luckily for Catesby and his contemporaries, "Virginia was the Place, as I had relatives there," he explained, "which suited most with my Convenience to go." It is there that we shall meet him again.

◀ 8. Whether formal or informal, a garden was no garden at all without flowers.

II

Virginia, the Royal Colony

I N THE BEGINNING no one knew how vast Virginia really was. It covered most of the North American continent claimed by England, true, but no one could describe it in terms of square miles or say he had seen its farthest boundaries. In fact, after a century and a half of colonization, Thomas Lee could only guess at what lay to the west. Reporting to the Board of Trade in 1750, he located Virginia on the east by "the Great Atlantic Ocean . . . by North Carolina to the South, by Maryland and Pennsylvania to the North, and by the South Sea to the West, including California."

The anchor end of this huge sweep of land is easier to comprehend. Known as tidewater Virginia, this region, carpeted by trees and fields, stretches westward toward the Virginia foothills and is drained by rivers that empty into the Chesapeake Bay. From the first, for the men who owned and worked its plantations, Virginia *was* Tidewater. For Jamestown's founders—"The Adventurers in England and Ancient Planters in Virginia"—the sights of the new continent centered on the

◀ 9. A show of tulips seen year after year in the Governor's Palace gardens.

19

James River and in the sounds and scents on each side of its wandering banks. They explored the Potomac, the Rappahannock, and the York, but when the land began to rise into the Piedmont, the Blue Ridge, and then the lovely valley of the Shenandoah—well, that could await the restless, the venturesome, and the second comers.

The soil and the climate of the Tidewater, the broad arable lands between the tidal streams that flowed into a network of bays and formed a magnificent system of waterways and natural harbors—these, plus tobacco, soon made Virginia the most populous of all England's colonies. The shores of the Tidewater along lower Chesapeake Bay, and inland the marshes, swamps and savannas—acre upon acre of tall waving marsh grass—all teemed with wild fowl. The scent of wild bloom floated across the water, and here and there was the rolling song of a bird all scarlet, the wing flash of a bird all blue. Upstream, tall trees, some with flowers resembling a tulip, and the white flowers of understory trees, brightened the dense forest. There was an impression of a waiting stillness, as of heavy noons, and a virgin verdancy, a depth of greenness such as the settlers had never known. Strangest of all came men "creeping upon all foures from the Hills, like Beares, with their Bowes in their Mouthes."

The Indians had either to be made into friends or exterminated. Disease, an enemy more subtle and deadly, took half the settlers of Jamestown the first year. The lack of food was an immediate problem, although summer rainfall kept vegetation lush and growing. And the economic pressure to find and develop some natural resource that would lend itself readily to trade—a precious metal was the great hope—was of first importance to the backers of the colony.

Actually, if we can accept the massacres of 1622 and 1644 as the price of his dispossession, the Indian turned out to be more help than hindrance. He knew the land and, however reluctantly, shared his knowledge. He had marked out every road-to-be with a trail, and he had gardens that grew strange new plants, among them Indian corn and a plant that he dried, put into a pipe, and smoked—a native weed he called *uppowoc* or *apooke*.

The colonists were already making their own glass and bricks when, in 1610, one of the London gentlemen and adventurers, John Rolfe, arrived in Jamestown. The school history books make much of John Rolfe's marriage to the Indian "princess" Pocahontas, but his memory deserves better. He was the man with an idea that was to prove a magic wand.

10. The tobacco plant *(Nicotiana tabacum)*. Tobacco growers "top" the flower bud long before it opens into its pink-flowered bloom, as this stray plant has done.

Rolfe knew the weed the Indians smoked, not as uppowoc or apooke, but as tobacco. For that matter, all Europe knew tobacco by 1610. Introduced by the Spaniards in 1552 and prized first as a cure-all herb, smoking it had become a rite in Paris, London, Madrid, and Rome, despite the fulminations of the churchmen and kings. Englishmen, among others, were planting tobacco in their gardens.

Sir Walter Raleigh, again as the school books tell us, had popularized smoking in the best circles of London as early as 1586, a generation before Rolfe's advent in Jamestown. What the books often fail to note, however, is that Raleigh's tobacco was presented to him by that master sea rover, Sir Francis Drake, who had captured it from a Span-

11. Flowering dogwood proclaims the spring.

ish galleon in the West Indies. Even earlier, Sir John Hawkins had brought tobacco to England from Florida.

In Virginia Rolfe found a kind of tobacco growing wild, one which had escaped from cultivation by the Indians, but it was too strong and bitter to suit his taste. Botanists were to identify it as *Nicotiana rustica,* a hybrid between two South American species. The Spanish tobacco popular in Europe was far milder, sweeter, and more fragrant. Rolfe decided that if the latter, a tropical variety to be known as *Nicotiana tabacum,* could be cultivated profitably in Virginia, that fact might be worth more than all the gold of the Incas.

With the help of a friendly shipmaster, he obtained some seeds of *Nicotiana tabacum* from the Spanish colony at Caracas, Venezuela, and from Trinidad. Experimenting in the growing and curing of the tropical plant near Jamestown, he founded within a few years an industry that was to work changes of greater and more lasting scope than those of all the century's wars.

The tobacco Rolfe found in Virginia grew "not fully a yard above the ground" and had short, coarse leaves. That introduced by Rolfe had long, broad leaves of finer texture and grew six to nine feet tall. He mastered the art of curing it, and the tobacco boom was on at Jamestown. Not even King James could check it, although he condemned smoking as "lothsome to the eye, hatefull to the Nose, harmefull to the braine, dangerous to the Lungs."

James shipped mulberry trees and silk worms to Jamestown, forced colonists to plant the trees, and offered "a Reward of Fifty Pounds of Tobacco for a Pound of Silk." Some silk, also cloth, was produced with scant enthusiasm; the colony was "dispersed all about, planting tobacco," too busy to be worrying about worms or such details as "the church downe, the palizado's broken, the bridge in pieces, the well of fresh water spoiled." The pink-flowered, light green-leafed *Nicotiana tabacum* sprang up even in the streets and the marketplace.

One man's labor with tobacco was worth six times his labor with wheat, the old wheelhorse of farm crops. Cured tobacco was easier to ship back to England, and there traders were crying for more and more of it to sell in Europe, a tobacco-hungry market to be wrested from Spain merely by supplying Virginia tobacco in plenty. By 1629, the James River Valley and Accomack Peninsula could count well over 2,500 English settlers—and at least one acre of tobacco for every two, including women and children. The plantations extended well up the James River. In another twenty years, tobacco was being planted along the Rappahannock and the Potomac. Still another twenty years, and the colony numbered 40,000, including the eventful addition of nearly 2,000 Negroes, some of whom were indentured servants, the rest slaves. Forty thousand tons of tobacco were annually to be tamped into Virginia hogsheads before cultivation of the "joviall weed" declined.

The settlers were overwhelmingly English, and Royalists, which was a sharp distinction from Puritan New England. James I had passed on, Charles I had lost his head to Cromwell, and how little parliamentary reform appealed to the Tidewater was demonstrated when Charles II was restored to the throne. The colonists proclaimed him king in Virginia before London hailed him as England's ruler. Charles, in gratitude, had his new coins engraved to show that his kingdom now embraced England, Scotland, Ireland, and Virginia.

Amid the gaiety and color of the English court tobacco was not forgotten either. Emigrants were encouraged to indenture themselves to a landowner who paid for their passage and to work off their debts over a period of four to seven years as his "indentured servant." That service performed, the free man might then buy his own acres of Virginia soil.

Owning land was no small reward to England's farmworkers. As to working off a debt in another's service, that seemed a fair and honorable bargain. To Virginia they came, the men and women of rural England, the blue-eyed, fair-haired people who picked in the apple orchards of Herefordshire or in the hop fields of Kent. Artisans, plowmen, laborers, women who could sew, cook, and "manage"—solid English stock.

Such was the pattern of life firmly established as the eighteenth century began. Aside from Williamsburg and the small port villages, the royal colony was wholly rural. Ships, billowing sails, could put in at countless harbors; the network of waterways allowed them to dock right at the larger planters' doors. Every large house faced upon a river and had its wharf. The principal roads to these wharves were the tobacco roads over which were pulled, by horses or oxen, the huge hogsheads of tightly packed tobacco leaves.

The plantations of Virginia's country gentlemen were worlds of their own, directed with the same taste and ability as those of English squires or lords of the manor. Apart from salt, spices, molasses, tea, and coffee, the land furnished everything. Timber, iron ore, and brickmaking clays were the raw materials for their carpenters, masons, wheelwrights, coopers, and blacksmiths. Many a large plantation had

▶

12. Mark Catesby planted three pink dogwoods in John Custis's garden.

its shoemakers, its spinners and weavers, its seedsmen, gardeners, brewers, bakers, and cooks, "within themselves."

The planter loved the countryside, although he bled the soil for tobacco. He loved horse racing, cockfighting, gambling, good food, and rare old wines. For schooling he sent his sons to the College of William and Mary, or to England, and it was not uncommon for one son of each plantation family to live in England to represent its tobacco interests.

Elegance increased with wealth. Georgian-style mansions facing the river highways came to dominate the Tidewater as the great country houses dominated the English scene. By mid-century, some 330 ships and 3,000 sailors were employed in the Virginia tobacco trade. Berthing alongside wharves of individual planters, the incoming ships unloaded books, pictures, fine pottery, clothes, and silver plate in exchange for the now "Imperial Weed" they would take home. Life for the plantation owner, like Rolfe's tobacco, was "as strong, sweet and pleasant as any under the sun."

I turn to the Reverend Hugh Jones for a summing up of plantation life during the early 1700s. Professor of mathematics at the College of William and Mary, a chaplain of the House of Burgesses, and later pastor of a country parish, Jones was born in England's Herefordshire near where I was born; so when, in his *The Present State of Virginia,* he likens some aspects there to life in Herefordshire, what he describes makes me feel akin to him. My native shire was slow to change.

> The gentlemen's seats are of late built for the most part of good brick, and many of timber very handsom . . . likewise the common planters live in pretty timber houses . . . with timber also are built houses for the overseers and out-houses, among which is the kitchen apart from the dwelling house, because of the smell of hot victuals, offensive in hot weather. . . . The houses stand sometime two or three together; and in other places a quarter, half a mile, or a mile, or two, asunder, such as in the country in England.

He esteemed the "cyder" almost as good as that of Herefordshire, then famed as the best in England. He praised Virginia wool and noted that "they pull the down of their living geese and wild and tame ducks, wherewith they make the softest and sweetest beds." And of the large landowners he found their "habits, life, custom, computations, etc. . . . much the same as about London, which they esteem their home."

Williamsburg flourished. Settled in 1633 as an outpost for James-

13. The King's Arms Tavern kitchen garden is decorative as well as useful.

town against Indian attack, the original site, known as Middle Plantation, had contained behind its palisade a blockhouse, a smithy, a mill, a store or two, a brick church, and a few houses. The village changed little until the College of William and Mary was founded there in 1693. Five years later, the statehouse at Jamestown burned, and in 1699 the capital moved to Middle Plantation, renamed Williamsburg after the king. For eighty-one years, until Richmond became the capital of the state, Williamsburg was the social, cultural, and political center of Virginia.

Most of its public buildings were built not long after it became the capital. Although one of the smallest of the original colonial capitals, Williamsburg spoke for the most populous and extensive of all the North American colonies. The town was small but beautiful. Francis Nicholson, governor from 1698 to 1705, devised a plan for what he envisioned would become a green country town, spacious and elegant as befitted the seat of government. Beginning in front of the Wren Building at the College—built earlier, according to Hugh Jones, after a design by Sir Christopher Wren—Governor Nicholson laid out what Jones was to describe as "a noble street mathematically streight . . . just three quarters of a mile in length: at the other end of which stands the Capitol, a noble, beautiful, and commodious pile as any of its kind." Approach to the Governor's Palace was alongside a great green forecourt—Palace Green. Every householder was allotted at least a half-acre of land on which to set his house, garden, and orchard. In 1705 the law required every lot owner to build a fence around his lot to protect the gardens from stray horses and cattle.

How successfully Governor Nicholson's plan met the requirements of what was virtually a planters' capital is reflected by travelers' reports. One likened it to "a good Country Town in England," another as having "a great air of opulence . . . houses, equal in magnificence to many of our superb ones at St. James's . . . ," and added, "There are also very pretty garden spots in the town . . . the country surrounding is thickly overspread with plantations and the planters live, in a manner, equal to men of the best fortune." Over all, from the flagstaff atop the Capitol, waved the Great Union flag of Britain.

It all had a very English flavor, but the setting was different. What contemporaries said of the main building of the College, now the oldest academic building in English America, was true in principle of every house and garden throughout Virginia. The College, said Hugh Jones, was "adapted to the Nature of the Country by the Gentlemen there."

Virginians developed a type of house that showed its English origin, but bore the unmistakable hallmark of being Virginia-made. And that was true of gardens, as of all else. They were of the same language, but with a Virginia accent.

The gardens of Williamsburg—and we should look first at the larger gardens, for they probably influenced the others—were modeled after the English formal garden when formality was at its crest. The superb Palace garden, for which credit is due chiefly to Alexander Spotswood, governor from 1710 to 1722, contained many of the features to be seen at Hampton Court during the reign of William and Mary. Famous in its own day, and more famous now as one of the few examples either in America or Europe of early eighteenth-century garden art, the Palace garden bespoke the pattern of many plantation gardens, and indirectly of every garden in Williamsburg, since most small lots were laid out as plantations in miniature.

There were good reasons why Williamsburg's planners did not follow the craze for gardens blending with the landscape, which swept through England after William and Mary but did not begin to have wide influence in America until after the Revolution. The colonists, mindful that until recently a clearing in the virgin land had been essential to their own safety from Indian attacks, had no desire to make a feature of either "wildernesses" or "shrubberies" at their doors. Besides, the blueprint of the formal garden they had known "back home" was clear in mind, and they wanted their Virginia acres to remind them of England as they remembered it, as far as Nature allowed.

Nature in the Tidewater imposed many differences. The "dependencies"—kitchen, smokehouse, wellhead, slave quarters—had to be built separately at the side or rear of the main building and be comely enough to serve as garden features too. Shade trees had to be planted close in, shade being a necessity—exactly the opposite of the English need for light and sun. Arbors and shaded walks served as outdoor retreats.

The architectural features of the old formal garden—arbors, covered seats, topiary, and espaliered fruit trees—fitted the Virginia setting admirably. There was one additional feature, previously denied them, that transplanted Englishmen could enjoy. In England only lords of the manor and noblemen were free to rear pigeons. Now citizens of Williamsburg could have their own dovecotes and keep the tasty little birds in their own small yards, like chickens.

Once the pattern was set, tidewater gardeners were not concerned

14. Dependencies in tidewater Virginia were essential outbuildings. The outdoor kitchen and smokehouse adjacent to the Brush-Everard House.

with changing fashions in design, but in learning what plants they could grow most rewardingly. They created small town gardens that, to my mind, have never been surpassed, as fitting for town life today as they were two hundred years ago. There was no reason for them to stop growing box, which flourishes so abundantly in Virginia, simply because Queen Anne didn't like the smell of it. Williamsburg became and remained a box stronghold. Incidentally, the box also provided housewives with a smooth surface on which to dry sheets and the like, whereas "Quick-setted arbors and hedges agreed very ill with the ladies muslins."

Flower growing in every age and land has developed in a similar pattern: useful plants are grown before ornamentals, and the first to cultivate flowers are the rich, to be followed in due course by those of moderate means. Although records do not exist to show just how much of Williamsburg's smaller gardens was given over to flowers, it is safe to presume that in general they followed the rule that the proportion of flowers to vegetables and herbs increased with each householder's means. Leading citizens, such as the Custises and the Randolphs, grew flowers in higher ratio, of course: they had more land, more labor, and more money to permit experimentation, with its risk of failure. Small lot holders sensibly, if necessarily, waited for proved things.

We may also presume, however, that the man of small means in Williamsburg had the benefits, no less than his English counterpart, if later, of the forward strides being made in England by nurserymen and gardeners. By no means was all of the experimenting and risk-taking being done by the rich; everyman's garden was being eyed by a developing industry of which, in time, he was to become a favored customer.

Above all, a love of flowers and gardening was inborn with a people whose roots lay in England. I doubt if a ship arrived without packets of seeds or bulbs, roots, or cuttings of some favorite plants tucked into the baggage of newcomers. The maids of Jamestown, many of them prospective brides, I am sure had firm ideas of home gardens-to-be in the new land long before they set foot on its soil.

Five miles from future Williamsburg, in 1619, a round 3,000 acres of fertile land, with a "very green spring" of clear water, were set aside to be tilled for the support of the governor. About 1650, on a tract immediately adjoining, Governor Berkeley developed his estate, Green Spring, after the fashion of the estate of an English country gentleman. Besides the mulberry trees decreed by King James, Berkeley planted 1,500 fruit trees, built a hothouse for oranges, and laid out extensive rose gardens on a terraced sward. Far more extensive and elaborate than the gardens of the Governor's Palace in Williamsburg, yet to be built, those of Green Spring set a standard that challenged all future garden planners in the colony.

Seldom do historians make much mention of gardens, but those dealing with the early Tidewater's settlement do. They note the extensive orchards "with all sorts of English apples . . . of which they made great store of cider," and the garden flowers, roses especially, and clove gilliflowers, sweet-smelling herbs such as rosemary, sage, marjoram, and thyme. Robert Beverley, in his *The History and Present State of Virginia,* published in 1705, asks "Have you pleasure in a Garden?" and proceeds to show that the first gentlemen of Virginia did have, no less than the English squire. "For their Recreation," he wrote, "the Plantations, Orchards, and Gardens constantly afford 'em fragrant and delightful Walks." He found most surprising the entertainment Virginians derived from "the Beauty of a Bed of Flowers."

Governor Berkeley was, undoubtedly, the most ambitious and, with the means at his disposal, the most prominent of the first great garden creators in Virginia. A garden is the most ephemeral of the arts, and Green Spring does not survive today. But Berkeley was the forerunner of a flower-loving gentry that included Governors Nicholson and Spotswood, the son of the founder of Westover plantation, William Byrd II, and in town such leading figures as John Custis and John Randolph.

These men brought the same zest, the same curiosity to their plantings as did that small band of pioneering professionals in England, the Society of Gardeners. They gave to every form of garden art the same encouragement and patronage shown by members of the Royal Society, offering welcome and hospitality to every plant-loving stranger who came their way.

Among them, William Byrd II was as outstanding in Virginia as was his friend, Sir Hans Sloane, in London, whom he resembled in many ways. One among many leaders of a great century, he represented the cultivated Virginia landowner at his best. Educated in England, and from time to time going back for extended visits, he lived at Westover as squire and public servant "attached to the soil and knowing the people." Both London's ancient legal fraternity, the Inns of Court, and the Royal Society listed him as a member.

The Secret Diary, which Byrd, like Pepys, the English diarist, wrote

▶

15. Williamsburg became and remained a boxwood stronghold. The Ludwell-Paradise garden.

16. John Custis, Peter Collinson's "brother of the spade" and John Bartram's host in Williamsburg. (Courtesy of Washington and Lee University.)

in shorthand, is full of references to country matters. His *Natural History of Virginia* records what he saw through eyes accustomed to the English scene—like those of the Reverend Hugh Jones. His was the appraising eye that delighted in that "miracle of nature" the hummingbird, that noted the "whitish-yellow plumage of the crane" whose quill he found "fine for writing." With just such a quill, no doubt, he wrote of the animals and birds, the trees, "and still many other flowers unknown in Europe . . . which please travellers with their beauty."

Byrd knew firsthand the impressions of travelers. Westover, his elegant Georgian mansion on the banks of the James River, was open house to them. With its tulip poplars shading the river frontage, its walled garden and small box-enclosed flower beds within, and the fruit trees for which the master of Westover was famous, Westover was a bit of England in the New World. From a plantsman's viewpoint, John Clayton, clerk of Gloucester County, and John Custis of Williamsburg had finer gardens, but William Byrd best represented the inquiring spirit of a gentleman of the colony.

Like Byrd, Custis was educated ("bred," he called it) in England. A member of the House of Burgesses, he later served in the Council for twenty-two years. He was what the English called a magnificent amateur gardener. No man of his time was so active in introducing and acclimating to Williamsburg plants from "back home." In addition, Custis was a link with a trio of great gardeners of the later generation of Williamsburg's heyday: John Randolph, George Washington, and Thomas Jefferson. The three were of the new order of Virginia gentlemen who were closer to the New World than the Old, who thought as Virginians, not as Englishmen, yet who could differ politically, too, over what was best for the American future.

John Randolph (1727–1784) was the last king's attorney for the colony and the loyalist who went "home" to England when the debates over American grievances gave way to revolution. To his son Edmund, however, home was, and remained, Virginia. It was symbolized by the family homestead, Tazewell Hall, that stood just back of where Williamsburg Lodge is situated today. Only a third of a mile away was John Custis's garden; Custis and the Randolphs, close neighbors, must often have compared garden notes and experiences.

The famous gardeners' dictionary compiled by Philip Miller, while valuable in Virginia up to a point, was not wholly a reliable guide for cultivating plants in a climate different from that of England. So around 1765, John Randolph wrote the first American guide for kitchen gardening, modeling it on the pattern of Miller's. He called his new work *A Treatise on Gardening,* and added what was to prove a sadly ironic subtitle, "Adapted to the present State of our Climate." The loyalist king's attorney died in England, and *A Treatise on Gardening* was not published until about ten years after his death. The book served gardeners of Virginia through several editions.

George Washington often visited Williamsburg, the Tidewater's proud center of town life. His wife, Martha, the widow of John Custis's son, had close Williamsburg ties. Washington himself was a member of the House of Burgesses, a country gentleman among gentlemen.

17. "Tall trees, some with flowers resembling a tulip" (tulip poplar).

Just after his marriage, on a May day of 1759, the master of Mount Vernon ordered from his London agent a copy of *New Principles of Gardening* as a step toward making his country seat on the Potomac one of the first outstanding versions in America of the "new" English style of informal or naturalistic landscaping.

Thomas Jefferson, too, favored the open landscape rather than the traditional formal design when he began his garden at Monticello, and he employed the serpentine curve instead of the straight line for his flower-bordered paths around the lawn. Seeking to furnish the garden in 1778, Jefferson purchased seeds and plants from the gardener at Green Spring. Governor Berkeley, although dead a century, was still an influence.

Despite his range of other activities, Jefferson faithfully kept his *Garden Book* from 1766 to 1824. It is the story of his Monticello garden and his observations, as a squire of the Virginia countryside, on agriculture. He liked jotting down the same small details that gardeners the world over record habitually: a note of the April day his sweet Williams began to open; another on the July flower beds gay with snapweed and the mauve, red, and yellow pincushion heads of globe amaranth; and of the day he had cucumbers from the vegetable patch for dinner.

Remembering the impact that John Rolfe's tobacco had made on Virginia, and Philip Miller's cotton seed on Georgia, it is not surprising that the author of the Declaration of Independence counted among his important services the introductions of the olive tree and dry rice into South Carolina. "No occupation," wrote Jefferson in 1811, "is so delightful to me as the culture of the earth, and no culture comparable to that of the garden." I am sure that every explorer and lover of *flora virginica* would have agreed with him.

III

Exploring Flora Virginica

T
O PLANTSMEN SEEKING TO TAP
the verdant wealth of England's North
American colonies, *flora virginica* was
the symbol of an El Dorado, a land of
floral abundance. Of about 8,000 plants since
identified as native to the eastern United States,
no more than a half-dozen were being cultivated
in England at the time Jamestown was settled.
When the Revolution intervened and Williamsburg ceased to be Virginia's capital, the total was
around 600 migrants from the American wilds
rerooted in English gardens.

The lure of *flora virginica* drew to Virginia an
oddly selfless breed of men—plant explorers.
They discovered, roving the Tidewater and following its streams inland to the Blue Ridge
and the valleys and mountains of the southern
Appalachians, one of the richest and most extensive floras in the world. During weeks of sailing,
England-bound shipmasters were asked to han-
dle with care the precious seeds and roots and
tubs of living plants formerly known only to the
Indians. In London, many a man's fingers

◀ 18. Carolina jessamine with its fragrant
yellow flowers adorns this picket fence.

39

Photo by Thomas L. Williams

trembled when he was able at last to open a fold of paper and spread wonderingly over his palm new seeds from 3,000 miles away. Thousands of letters were written by quill and candlelight as growers of these migrants shared their knowledge.

Who was first to introduce what, first to coax it to grace his garden, is hard to say with certainty today. The records that survive, however, illuminate a story of exploration rare in history books cluttered with wars.

The early plant hunters did not need to go far afield. "Of Spontaneous Flowers they have an Unknown Variety," was one report from the Tidewater. By 1700, probably a hundred and fifty importations were growing in English gardens. No one was more zealous in those early introductions than the Tradescants, father and son, each of whom served as royal gardener to Charles I. They also maintained their own garden and obtained rare plants from all sorts of travelers. John Tradescant II himself visited the Tidewater on a collecting mission. The catalogue of their garden listed in 1656 an impressive array of *flora virginica.*

The Tradescants' harvest included the Virginia creeper and Tradescant's Aster (later called by *The Botanical Magazine* the original Michaelmas daisy), now the common name in England for the vast tribe of asters. They also brought in *Tradescantia virginiana* or spiderwort; coneflowers and columbine, bee balm (or bergamot), the common evening primrose—which Londoners call the Virginia tree primrose—phlox, lupines, and goldenrod. These today are among the English gardener's old-fashioned flowers, the standbys of the grand herbaceous border and the hardy perennials of the small cottage garden.

Others than the Tradescants domesticated Tidewater flowers, but who first picked a Jamestown lily we do not know. Nor do we know who sent the red lobelia, said to have been growing along every "branch" or creek and which was named the Cardinal flower because of its crimson likeness to a cardinal's robe.

We do know that the dawning of the eighteenth century brought to Virginia plantsmen who were more than collectors; they were true botanical explorers. The wayside flowers were fairly well known by then. Finding the unusual demanded lonely expeditions of weeks or months, meticulous combing of a wild terrain as little known as the moon's. There were no texts or precedents; hundreds of green growing things were without classification or name—pure mysteries. Foot,

19. Spiderwort, *Tradescantia virginiana,* named for the Tradescants, John the Elder and John the Younger, royal gardeners in turn to King Charles I.

horseback, and canoe were the means of travel. The night's campfire under the stars was the inn; Indians, bears, malarial mosquitoes, and rattlesnakes were regular company, but the next day usually held forth the excitement of discovery.

These dedicated pioneers of our gardens did not grow rich in their finds. Reward lay in things as simple as the color, texture, and perfume of a wildflower, in the song of a strange bird, and the constant rustle of the forest. Lover of this wild country, the plant hunter methodically labeled his spray *flora virginica,* pressed, packed, and later sent it by sailing ship to the other side of the world. But he conveyed with it none of the glorious exhilaration of his discovery. He was no storyteller.

Yet, he was a lucky man, and knew it, for never before or since was the time so ripe for his kind. In the upper circles of Georgian England —aristocratic, elegant—the rare new plant from El Dorado was more prized than a jewel. Scientists of the Royal Society wrote learnedly of the floral migrants; gentlemen of distinction discussed them at the coffee house; the king and queen took pride in their green thumbs, and in their "Exoticks."

First of the dedicated plant explorers was doubtless John Banister, who knew Williamsburg as Middle Plantation. A young missionary of Protestant England, he had already traveled in the West Indies and Brazil before Henry Compton, the bishop of London whom we will recall as Queen Mary's tutor, sent him to Virginia. Banister was certainly the Tidewater's first priest, botanist, and entomologist rolled into one.

Twenty-eight years old, he explored far beyond the white man's settled lands for over fourteen years, collecting, cataloguing, and making drawings of insects, shells, and fossils as well as plants. Back to the bishop, for his famous Fulham Palace garden, he sent the fringe tree, the sweet bay magnolia, and the sweet gum. During his first two years in Virginia he compiled two catalogues of Virginia plants, one with drawings. Later, he added a collection of dried plants that was acquired eventually by Sir Hans Sloane and now reposes in the British Museum.

Up the James River and the York, up their tributary creeks, up streams yet to be mapped (one later named for him, the Banister River, crosses the Virginia-North Carolina line) Banister roamed, botanizing as he went. He was one of the first, if not *the* first, plant explorer to light his campfire high in the virgin forests of the Blue Ridge. There on the Peaks of Otter, 200 miles from the sea, he met his death on a plant-hunting expedition.

Perhaps as a memorial, the bishop of London printed Banister's *Catalogue of Virginia Plants,* the first known work of its kind and the cornerstone for the work of those following. A lesser-known memorial was a letter of Edward Randolph, surveyor general of customs, who was at Jamestown not long after Banister's death trying to hurry up the dispatch of more Virginia seeds to England. There seems to have been a pause in the flow and London was growing impatient. The surveyor general was able to send only a paper of seeds that he identified as black haws, and "some sena, which the indians bruise and putting the Juce in warm water to make them vomitt." He explained, "Mr. Banister the chiefe florist being dead here is no man understands the nature of names of the many hundred growing here different from those in England."

It was not until Williamsburg became the capital that the gap left by John Banister began to be filled by two young men who crossed the ocean separately but became lifelong friends and kindred souls. They were John Clayton, son of Sir John Clayton, who became the attorney general for Virginia, and Mark Catesby, to whom "Virginia was the Place" most suited to him to go. His sister was the wife of William Cocke, Williamsburg physician and later secretary to the colony. Young Catesby, his way to make, added himself to the doctor's household.

Clayton and Catesby were plantsmen all their lives. Each produced a major work, but there the similarities between them end. From the books that resulted from their work, we can assume that Clayton saw the world in prose, Catesby in poetry. Clayton won the respect of the professional; Catesby delighted the amateur.

John Clayton came to Virginia with his father in 1705 and in due course became clerk of Gloucester County, an office he held for fifty-one years, seldom wandering west of his neighborhood there near the Chesapeake Bay. All of his leisure, which plainly he had in abundance, was spent collecting and growing plants in his botanical garden at Windsor on the Piankatank River in what is now Mathews County. Of the man himself, for all his long life (he died at eighty-eight), we know disappointingly little. The Williamsburg surgeon, Dr. John Galt, found him witty in conversation. The Indians liked him because they said he listened and learned from them. Thomas Jefferson revered him as one who "enlarged the botanical catalogue as much as almost any man who has lived." But Clayton is best known, as he would probably prefer, through *Claytonia virginica,* the common spring beauty or mayflower that honors his name, and whose white, sometimes pink-flushed flowers carpet the moist thickets and woods throughout the eastern United States.

The middle districts of the Tidewater were Clayton's chief hunting ground. He send seeds and plants to Catesby and others who were friends by correspondence. His herbarium specimens, which he sent to Gronovius in Holland, that eminent Dutch botanist used as the basis of his *Flora Virginica,* printed (in two parts) in 1739 and 1743. Clayton meanwhile doubled his roll of collector by becoming a systematic botanist, and the revisions of the *Flora's* second edition of 1762, enlarged by Collinson and other English botanists, were largely Clayton's work.

The new edition was one of the first complete botanical manuals of the New World, and there was a certain justice in John Clayton's being

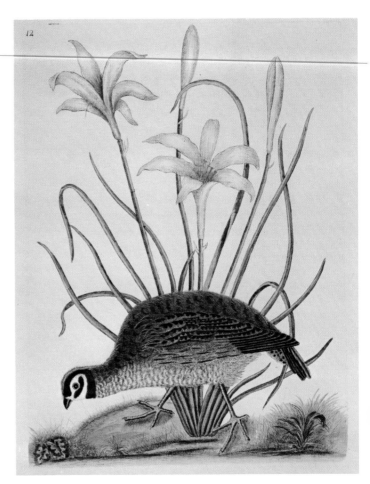

20. Mark Catesby pictured his "American partridge," or quail, beside the Jamestown (Atamasco) lily.

the man to bring it all together—to sum up the work of all the collectors since Jamestown was settled. He had spent more years than anyone else in gathering and growing tidewater flowers. Clayton would hardly be remembered but for Gronovius, who gave him full credit for his contribution to *Flora Virginica*. Clayton's own two hand-written volumes, with many drawings and a second herbarium, were destroyed in 1787 along with the county records in the burning of the courthouse.

Mark Catesby had no wish to be only botanist and collector, nor to confine himself solely to collecting within a limited area. All Nature was his province. His was the wide view gained after ten years of roving—seven in Virginia (1712–1719), then, after an interval back home, three years in the Carolinas, Florida, and the Bahamas. His friendships with plantsmen on both sides of the water were face-to-face, and the wild he knew also face-to-face, as only an artist could.

While in Virginia, Catesby had no thought of writing a book. He busied himself with sketching plants, birds, fish, any wild thing that took his fancy, with collecting and sending plants and seeds to England, and with visiting the Indians. Later he was to write home, "To the Hospitality and Assistance of these Friendly Indians, I am much indebted, for I not only subsisted on what they shot, but their First Care was to erect a Bark Hut, at the Approach of Rain to keep me and My Cargo from Wet." He helped John Clayton and John Custis with their gardens and at Westover learned that William Byrd, though widely knowledgeable of the country, was not quite the green thumb he pretended to be.

Returning to England in 1719, Catesby found that his drawings tended to enhance his growing reputation as a plant hunter. Botanists considered him one "pretty well skill'd in Natural history who designs and paints in water colours to perfection." With the blessing of the Royal Society, and financial help from individual sponsors, he was sent on his expedition into the deep South.

Catesby returned intent on writing, illustrating, and printing what was to be his *Natural History,* a task of twenty years. They were lean years for him. To support himself he worked in the gardens of his friend, Thomas Fairchild, and in those of other London nurserymen. His meager means did not permit him to pay for engravings of his paintings, so he took lessons in etching in order to do the work himself. A friend, the great botanical illustrator, Georg Dionysius Ehret, contributed two etchings; still another good friend, Peter Collinson, helped by lending a considerable amount of money without interest so the hopeful author might market his work without falling prey to booksellers.

Catesby liked to paint his subjects from life "fresh and just gather'd." In the main he did so. He worked from some of his original sketches, and through Clayton, Custis, Byrd, and other friends in America he received a continuing supply of plants and seeds. These supplemented the stocks of his nurserymen employers and gave him a whole gallery of fresh flowers from the New World. His favorites among them were, presumably, those he included in his books: the Jamestown lily, the mountain laurel, sweet shrub, and the pink flowering dogwood. This last was lost to cultivation for a hundred years; the trees he had planted in Clayton's and Custis' gardens died, and for long a pink dogwood was thought to be a freak or a myth. But Catesby had his original sketch, which showed it to be neither.

The first volume of his *History* came out in 1731, preceding the second volume by fourteen years. Catesby's own hand had colored the prints of the 220 engraved plates of the two volumes. As 156 sets were printed, that means he had laboriously colored 34,320 prints. An Appendix was added to the volumes in the spring of 1747, and on the April day it was completed a vast sigh of relief must have been breathed in the home of many a friend. Peter Collinson wrote to the great Linnaeus that "Catesby's noble work is finished."

He called this work of love *The Natural History of Carolina, Florida, and the Bahama Islands,* but actually it embraced most of Britain's portion of what we know today as the American South. Catesby made sure that his helpers in the Tidewater were remembered with copies.

He was now sixty-four, a distinguished elder among North American naturalists in England. His unrivaled firsthand experience both in field and garden, his friendship with notables on both sides of the ocean, gave him a unique authority. He was the only plant-wise Englishman able to convey with complete understanding the differences between the English and the Virginia scene. Those who saw his illustration of the quail (or American partridge, as he called it) beside the Jamestown lily knew at once the flower's habit and from Catesby's description could see it growing, abundant and strictly local—by the acre or not at all—"where in particular places the pastures are as thick sprinkled with them and Martagons, as Cowslips and Orchises are with us in England."

It was natural that plantsmen going to Virginia or returning from there should call on the grand old man. We have a glimpse of an afternoon when Peter Kalm went to see him before embarking on his own travels into North America, and found there also Dr. John Mitchell, the naturalist-physician for whom the partridgeberry, *Mitchella repens,* was named. The three talked nearly the whole afternoon. Catesby, tall, thin, usually taciturn, was as communicative and affable as the day William Byrd greeted him at Westover with cakes and a bottle of canary, then took him into a nearby swamp to look for the nest of a hummingbird.

Mark Catesby, along with other ardent gardeners, busied himself in acclimatizing American plants, including such stalwart Virginians as the yellow-berried hawthorn, sweet shrub, stewartia, and the catalpa

21. Mountain laurel, named *Kalmia latifolia* for Peter Kalm.

tree—which now grows on each side of Williamsburg's long Palace Green. *Aster grandiflorus* was indisputably another Catesby introduction. Known first as Catesby's starwort, it flowered in England for the first time in 1720. Robert Furber, the nurseryman, included it among the twenty-five American plants in his catalogue, adding the footnote that it came by Mr. Catesby, "a very curious gentleman from Virginia."

There were better collectors, better botanists, better artists than Catesby, but in sum total no one contributed as much. His *Natural History* was the outstanding work of its kind before the American Revolution and later influenced the career of another artist and lover of the American wild, John James Audubon. Catesby revived the interest in England aroused by Banister in the variety and beauty of American shrubs and trees and warmed Peter Collinson's heart for them. How this, in turn affected John Bartram, Philadelphia's great botanist-collector, we shall see.

22. Poppy anemones beside the ball-and-chain
device for a self-closing gate.

"Curious" was a word used to describe many of the garden lovers of that day. Collinson used it of John Custis, leading some now to think of Custis as an eccentric. But "curious" was applied in the old sense of ingenious, studious, having curiosity and the interest of the connoisseur. Of all such, Peter Collinson was among gardeners perhaps the most curious of all. Certainly in the story of *flora virginica* he was outstanding among those "Encouragers of Gardening" in England who exchanged new plants for old. His chief aides in that traffic were John Bartram and John Custis, his "brothers of the spade," as Collinson called his gardening friends.

Collinson himself, a Quaker, tells us that at a very early age he was taught to love plants and gardens. This was a precept of George Fox, founder of the Society of Friends, to be observed as carefully as the injunction to practice frankness and fair dealing. Collinson lived his life accordingly. His first concern after his family was the linen draper business in London he inherited from his father; his second was a love for plant life that he sought to express in the improvement of English gardens. He echoed Burke's belief that to be loved one's country must be made lovely, and helping to make England so became a lifetime ambition. Of his efforts he wrote, "I willingly undertook it [the work and expense] without the least gain of profit to myself in hope to improve or at least to adorn my country."

To that end he imported plants and seeds from all over the world—through the Jesuits, from far-off China, by way of St. Petersburg and "the Caravan." Because of Mark Catesby, however, he focused his interest on North America—corresponding with botanists, scientists, traders, and travelers. At the end of a day's business, he sat down to write his letters by quill pen with a patience almost inconceivable in our day of typewriters and dictaphones. For forty years he was the driving force that inspired the interchange of plants between the mother country and her American colonies. Collinson contributed immeasurably to the cultural life of early Virginia and all America. But for his help, Clayton's work would never have been so complete and Catesby's might have gone unpublished. Some biographers call Collinson the single most important person in Benjamin Franklin's life, the man responsible for his initial work with electricity and for its continuation.

They might say the same of Collinson's influence on John Bartram, most notable of all plantsmen who knew old Williamsburg as a way station on their journeys toward the rich Appalachian highlands. Bartram looked to Collinson for the support in England that made his great services possible. The two were allied for thirty-eight years. What together they did for the gardens of their countrymen has no parallel elsewhere or at any other time in garden history.

John Bartram was entirely self-taught, a Pennsylvania farmer who fell in love with a field daisy and forsook his plow to become, with Collinson's influence, Botanizer Royal in America under George III. Linnaeus acclaimed him the greatest natural botanist in the world. Traveling thousands of miles, often afoot, through unmapped, unsettled eastern America, alone or with his son William, he collected plants and seeds more diligently than anyone before or since. His single effort introduced into England between 150 and 200 plants. In return, Bartram's English friends sent back plants to grow in his garden beside the Schuylkill River, near Philadelphia, for likely introduction to America.

He made several journeys to the Shenandoah Valley of Virginia, which he called "my Kashmir." In 1738 he was in the Tidewater. Letters passing between the redoubtable trio of Collinson-Bartram-Custis on this visit give an idea of how the system of plant exchange worked. Collinson never could grasp the rigors of plant hunting in the wilderness, nor its dangers. Yet he was imaginative and useful in other ways. On the eve of Bartram's botanical tour of Virginia, Collinson asked him to provide himself with a fine suit of clothes, explaining:

> these Virginians are a very gentle, well-dressed people and look perhaps more at a man's outside than his inside . . . pray go very clean, neat, and handsomely dressed, to Virginia. Never mind thy clothes: I will send thee more another year.

Writing at length to John Custis, Collinson forewarned him of a visitor who might be mistaken for a plowman:

> I so much persuaded my self of such an Interestt in your Friendship you'l not Look att the Man but his Mind for my sake. His Conversation I dare say you'll find compensate for his appearance. . . . He comes to Visit your parts in serch of Curiosities. . . . He is imployed by a Sett of Noble Men (by my Recommendation) to Collect seeds & specimens of Rare plants, and he has been very successful in this affair which proceeds from His thorough knowledge in these Matters. Be so kind to give him a Little Entertainm't & Recommend Him to a Friend or Two of yours in the Country, for He does not Value [mind] riding 50 or 100 Miles to see a New plant. Pray Direct Him to the Umbrella Tree, this plant or Tree will make Him think his Journey worth Comeing. I have a further Desire in his waeting

23. Crape myrtle was one of the treasures that plantsmen received from far-off China.

on you, the Gardens of pensilvania are Well furnish'd with European Rarities possibly He may assist you with some plants that you Want & you may assist Them for I presume you have Vessills passing too & fro Often from one province to the Other. His name is John Bartram.

Custis was delighted with Bartram, who promised to send him some wanted plants. Later, Bartram confided to Collinson that he considered Byrd's Westover the finest seat in Virginia, John Clayton's garden the best furnished, and Custis's next. This appraisal might be interpreted that, to Bartram, Westover represented the best of the gardens maintained by a corps of gardeners, Clayton's the best botanical garden, and Custis's the gardener's garden. The three were as different in character as their owners.

Other letters that passed between Custis and Collinson from 1734 to 1746 add to our knowledge of the ups and downs of plant exchange. It was one thing for a plant hunter to come into Williamsburg with his haul of the trip, mosquito bitten, scratched by briars, skinned by rocks, unwashed and spent, if triumphant. It was another thing to get his precious finds packed or properly tubbed and down to the ship "in the nick of Time," happy that they "Look'd Exceeding Well," and with "great Hopes they'l come finely to hand." Two times out of three it did not work out that way.

The tubbed plants were often dead on arrival because at sea the captain and crew had more pressing duties than to tend such cargo. The temperature variations of the voyage took their toll. Surviving plants had to be nursed back to health in a climate very different from that of their nativity. It was a gamble which lived or which died. Seeds were easier to ship, but by no means guaranteed success, for we read from a Custis letter, "All the acceptable seeds you sent me never came up except a very few which came to nothing notwithstanding I kept 3 strong Nigros continually filling large tubs of water and put them in the sun and waterd plentifully every night, made shades and arbors all over the garden allmost; but abundance of things perishd; notwithstanding all the care and trouble . . . "

Custis, in his day, was the largest importer of European plants to the Tidewater. Having both time and money to devote to his hobby, he sought tirelessly to expand and better the selections available to Williamsburg gardeners of imported plants that were, as he put it, hardy and Virginia-proof. If he was partial in his labor (as a fine collection of lilacs might suggest) it may have been only that he shared the older English gardener's craze for greens.

In this, of course, he was not unique. As we have seen, the early colonists gave first place in their hearts to the old garden favorites of "back home," which to them was the England of the Stuarts, of William and Mary. Too, more than sentiment was attached to many of their garden treasures. The peony was valued for its healing powers; a syrup of rose petals eased sore throats; a brew of hollyhock was useful in voiding "Stones and gravel"; marigolds, in a hot drink, helped reduce fever, as every man, maid, master, and mistress knew.

The pioneers' devotion and respect for the tried and true plants of their forebears was to prove an annoying handicap to Collinson and others seeking to import plants rare to England. To the early settler, the rare *was* in England, not in the abundance of the new land. Aside from tobacco, and a few ornamental exceptions—coral honeysuckle for one, the sweet bay magnolia for another—there seemed no point in cultivating in the Tidewater flowers that thrived all around, wild and unattended like common weeds; and surely it would be silly to send weeds back home.

But in England the weeds of *flora virginica* were the rarities, and many doubly so. The Old World was rich in the flowers of spring and early summer, poor in those of the late summer and autumn. In the New World, by happy chance, that order was turned about: the wealth was of late summer and fall flowers. That heaven-sent coincidence was a fact that Collinson had endless trouble conveying to America until men such as Catesby, Clayton, Custis, and John Bartram became informed procurers. Later, in summing up, Collinson wrote:

> I used much importunity to very little purpose for the favour of the people was entirely the other way. What was common with them but rare with us they did not think worth sending. Thus I laboured in vain or to little purpose for some years and obtained but few seeds or plants, neither money nor friendship would tempt them.

Time has proved that commonly found plants, mostly wayside flowers of marsh and meadow and the first to catch a traveler's eye, are those that have endeared themselves to the average English gardener. The rarer beauties from remote spots have remained comparatively shy in cultivation and are more often found in the gardens of connoisseurs. The paradox is not without reason. Often the common plants possess a stamina and adaptability to change that the others lack, and, in the long run, everyman's flower must prove practical— hardy and undemanding as well as ornamental.

It was the plants with which Nature was most prodigal in the Tidewater that rooted deepest in English gardens, as the time-proved hardy

perennials of "home" rooted deepest in the gardens of Williamsburg. And from England the "weeds" of the New World, hybridized into floral hosts, went forth to Britain's farthest future colonies, to Australia, New Zealand, to wherever the Union Jack whipped in the wind.

The shift of the capital in 1780 from Williamsburg to Richmond, the town William Byrd II had founded at the falls of the James River, marked the end of colonial Virginia as surely as did the Declaration of Independence. It also marked the end of the era of great plantsmen, of the "Procurers of Plants and Encouragers of Gardening" for whom the tiny capital had been both base and crossroads. John Custis and Mark Catesby both had died in 1749. Peter Collinson died in 1768, Philip Miller in 1771, John Clayton in 1773, and John Bartram in 1777, the same year as Carolus Linnaeus, the father of botanical science.

Their era died with them, or did it?

Today, in historic Williamsburg, where the trees, shrubs, and flowers being grown are mostly those known to eighteenth-century plantsmen and gardeners, you will see living results of these men's life work. The restored gardens present a bit of old England in America that has largely vanished from the landscape of England itself.

And in England today you may see the paralleling paradox of all sorts of weeds from colonial North America (as "improved" by generations of gardeners) occupying prized places in the modern English garden. Among them: sunflowers and the evening primrose; bergamot, phlox, and the vast family related to the black-eyed Susan; asters and goldenrod. These and others have so long been the English gardener's favorites that he classes them among his land's own stalwarts that colonists took to America, such as sweet Williams, Canterbury bells, marigolds, and daffodils.

The shades of William and Mary, and Governor Berkeley too, must smile with us, knowing that what William Cobbett wrote in *The American Gardener* in 1816 is still true (except that a queen now rules England):

> A yellow flower, called the *"Plain-weed,"* which is the torment of the neighbouring [American] farmer, has been, above all the plants in this world, chosen as the most conspicuous ornament of the front of the King of England's grandest palace, that of Hampton-Court, where, growing in a rich soil to the height of five or six feet, it, under the name of *"Golden Rod,"* nods over the whole length of the edge of a walk, three quarters of a mile long and, perhaps, thirty feet wide, the most magnificent, perhaps, in Europe.

◀ 24. Black-eyed Susan, one of North America's treasures
that plantsmen sent "home" to England.

IV

Rediscovering A Tradition

I T WAS THE GOLDENROD that one August morning in Williamsburg a decade or more ago brought home an old truth to me: flowers are not dead curios. They are the immortals, the living things that tie together our forefathers' yesterdays and our todays, as they will link our own time with endless tomorrows. America was then new to me. I was feeling much the stranger, as a visitor in the Governor's Palace, when the old and familiar of my childhood in England was suddenly before my eyes, and it was as though I were home.

It so happens that the house in which I grew up was built during the reign of Queen Anne, the sister of Queen Mary, and that my mother, too, was an eager gardener and arranger of flowers. She loved to keep a great bunch of asters and goldenrod in a copper bowl on the oak chest in our hall every autumn. And there in the Governor's Palace, even as my mother might have arranged them, again I saw the tall stalks of goldenrod, not as a wild nuisance of the American fields but as beloved flowers on parade.

◀ 25. The formal dining room in the Governor's Palace. A portrait of King James I looks down on the dining table and the double pagoda-top épergne filled with fruit. Highbush cranberry is massed in a Chinese porcelain jar in the fireplace.

I looked upon the golden sprays as upon old friends stretching their hands out for mine. They seemed to talk, and why not? They alone of all the prized furnishings and portraits of the Palace were alive and personally meaningful. They were no different intrinsically from the flowers of my mother's garden than if the arranger had actually picked them there; they were, as well, or might have been, the goldenrods of Queen Mary, or those that Philip Miller had known as "very great Ornaments."

Who had accorded those weeds of America's fields what I, English-reared, regarded as their rightful place of distinction in the Governor's Palace?

It was Mrs. Louise B. Fisher who, as I learned, had restored golden-rod to its proper position. She was responsible also for the large bouquets I saw in the Governor's Palace. But finding Mrs. Fisher was almost like trying to run down a will-o'-the-wisp. She seemed to be here, there, everywhere, always on the way to somewhere else a stride ahead of me.

Eventually I caught up with her—in the first pause of her busy day—sitting upright. Tall, slim, and white haired, reticent I guessed, but alive to questioning, she was delighted that to me the goldenrod was not a weed. As a first impression unchanged over the years since, I remember that she looked as though she had stepped out of a bandbox despite her early morning work with more flowers than most of us arrange throughout the year.

In time, I got to know her well. Her work at Williamsburg had covered twenty-three years when she retired in 1956. Before that period, flower arrangers wed to rules and to this "school" or that were wont to smile tolerantly at the bouquets of housewives whose only rules were their own taste and a love for the flowers they displayed in their homes. Almost singlehandedly Louise Fisher revived forgotten eighteenth-century traditions—the same that had inspired my mother's bouquets in our Queen Anne home—to win lasting recognition that the rule-free arrangements of home and hearth are perhaps the oldest of all forms of the floral arts, the form in which the arranger is as free as the birds to express herself as she will.

Louise and Professor John Fisher came to Williamsburg in 1930, he to head the Department of Modern Languages at the College of William and Mary, she to bring with them as much of her garden in Ashland, Virginia, as she possibly could. They arrived with one truck of furniture and two trucks of plants to grace their new home on Duke of Gloucester Street. The restoration of Williamsburg had just begun. In the fall of 1932 the Raleigh Tavern opened. The following spring she became a hostess there. Aware that nothing serves better than flowers to lend a touch of home and welcome, she was pleased to be invited to arrange them regularly in several of the Tavern's rooms.

She soon learned that one hazard of being a hostess in a historic place is the question that some visiting authority, who already knows the answer, likes to ask. Why did she use dahlias, and why did she include grapefruit in a bowl of fruit, when neither were known in colonial days? Momentarily taken aback, and by nature as curious a gardener as any Byrd or Custis, she resolved to find out. The Research Department, devoted to the restoration, busy enough piecing together the jigsaw puzzle of old Williamsburg buildings, was happy to leave to her the rediscovery of eighteenth-century uses of flowers. Meanwhile, the Raleigh Tavern bouquets were so well liked that she was asked to arrange others in the Palace and the Wythe House. Later, the Brush-Everard House was added to her floral tour.

The expanded work created an immediate need for a cutting garden; in addition, Mrs. Fisher was told to draw as she wished upon a woodland owned by Colonial Williamsburg for wildflowers and foliage. What she had happily accepted as an extra duty then became a full-time job of undreamed consequences, for the old-time bouquets had to reflect the restored capital's bygone way of life as authentically as the wall coverings, furnishings, and other antiques.

Exactly what flowers and foliage had been used in those bouquets of a bygone age? How and where were they arranged and placed? Exactly what containers were most preferred by the colonial ladies?

Finding answers to those and other complex questions, answers that would hold under the scrutiny of critics, meant a tireless combing of records, months of correspondence, long evenings of plowing through old books after the day's work of cutting and arranging and placing was done.

From standard works such as Parkinson's *Paradisi* and Philip Miller's *Gardeners Dictionary,* a plant list was compiled. The cutting garden was established gradually, guided by the research, until it now includes more than two hundred kinds of annuals, perennials, bulbs, and shrubs that were certainly known to English and American gardeners of the eighteenth century. Necessarily, some of the flowers now grown are modern varieties of the original plants; the only moderns chosen, however, are those that are of colonial lineage and most nearly resemble their ancestors. A visitor may look in vain for dahlias and petunias, for instance, because those useful decorative flowers would not be recognized by the housewives of old Williamsburg.

Study of the same standard garden works and scattered references in travelers' reports and other writings of the period made it evident that the English—and Virginians, too—had as strong a love for showing off flowers in the home as for growing them outdoors. Flowers were displayed in the house wherever space could be found for them, from the floor up to the chimneypiece (or mantel)—with one exception. Although "never" and "always" are dangerous words to use in detailing the customs of any bygone age, it was not then customary to set flowers on the dining room table.

It is enlightening to take a closer look at this pleasant old custom of strewing flowers everywhere about the home. A good half-century before Jamestown was founded, the custom had taken firm hold, for practical as well as decorative reasons, upon England's housewives. Sweet-smelling plants were believed to prevent pestilence, and besides, they kept the house smelling fresh and clean. The fragrance of a flower or herb was as highly valued as its beauty.

Travelers' reports speak of how lavishly both were prized. The Dutch physician, Levinus Lemnius, visiting England in 1560, noted:

> Their chambers and parlours strawed over with sweet herbs refreshed mee; their noesgays finely intermingled with sundry sorts of fragraunte flowers, in their bed-chambers and privy rooms, with comfortable smell cheered me up, and entirely delyghted all my senses. . . . Altho we do trimme up our parlours with greene boughes, freshe herbes or vine leaves, no nation does it more decently, more trimmely, nor more sightly than they doe in Englande.

Almost two hundred years later, Peter Kalm, the Swedish naturalist, wrote:

> The *English* ladies in general are much inclined to have fine flowers all the summer long, in or upon the chimneys, sometimes upon a table, or before the windows, either on account of their fine appearance, or for the sake of their sweet scent.

Kalm, too, recorded that flowers were gathered "both in the gardens and in the fields."

By widespread custom, potted plants and fresh flowers were set on window sills. "Chimneys," as the wide, open fireplaces were called, were embellished with greens or flowers during the summer because "A Chimney thus done doth grace a Room exceedingly." In early fall, certain flowers, commonly called everlastings, were harvested and dried "for Basons to adorn Rooms in the Winter Season." A bason, of course, was a basin or shallow bowl, one of the various types of favored containers to which we shall devote our next chapter.

Everlastings, dried by patient craftsmanship, that took the home stage after the frosts had set in and winter was knocking at our ancestral doors have come back into favor again. Mention dried flowers in most garden clubs nowadays and the debate will wax high. However, as one devoted to the faithful recreation of old customs, Louise Fisher could not afford to take sides in such arguments. Fresh flowers in colonial Williamsburg, as in England, were few in winter. The drying of blooms, seed pods, and leaves was a proudly practiced home art—an art all but lost to our own day. Mrs. Fisher was a trailblazer among those pioneers who revived it into what is now a small, thriving industry.

I say all but lost, because I have fond memories of flowers for winter being dried as an autumn routine in my own and neighboring English country houses. Potted plants furnished their quota of fresh blooms, as did the glass house; but the everlastings, preserved by knowing hands, had their places. Yellowed diaries and letters and the old books that Mrs. Fisher, attentive to her researches, read late into the night, made repeated references to the craft. They also mentioned a rare exception among garden flowers: the black hellebore whose large white flowers bloom in England before Christmas and often throughout January. Peter Collinson lovingly described it as the "Xmas Rose." Yet, even with it and other rarities at his disposal, Collinson paid tribute to the everlastings. The globe amaranth, a mainstay among them, was one of the plants he sent to John Custis at Williamsburg, followed by a careful note:

> I am much Delighted to heare you have your amaranthoides. It is a Real and I may say perpetual Beauty. If the flowers are gather'd in perfection and hung up with their Heads Downwards in a Dry shady Room, they will keep thear Colours for years and will make a pleasant Ornament to Adorn the Windows of your parlor or study all the Winter. I Dry great quantities for that purpose and putt them in flower potts and China basons and they make a fine show all the Winter.

Philip Miller recorded that everlastings were "brought to the Mar-

kets in great Plenty during the Winter Season," and he advised that "when their Stalks were put into Glasses with Sand, the Flowers would continue in Beauty till the Spring."

With pointers such as these, a wonderful variety of plant material upon which to draw, and a plant lover's instinctive know-how, Mrs. Fisher set out to follow the way of the old craft. From her cutting garden, the woodland preserve, and the surrounding free countryside Mrs. Fisher assembled her flowers, ferns, and grasses, her seed pods, ears of wheat and corn tassels, common weeds, and autumn leaves. It was no small task, this providing of plenty for winter, and one year the story got around that she had twelve college students helping her to scour the countryside over a fifty-mile radius. The fact was that she had only the temporary use of a station wagon and the help of a driver and an assistant for a few hours once or twice a week.

Occasionally there was a windfall. Once her assistant noticed armloads of purple blooms lying among the swaths of newly mown grass and weeds along the road from Williamsburg to Yorktown. The harvest was promptly transferred to the drying room and the plant identified as one of the ornamental alliums that had probably become naturalized. Later, a friend whose garden nearby was overrun with the plant, gave some bulbs to Mrs. Fisher for planting in the Williamsburg cutting garden. Popularly known as Yorktown onions, they have been there ever since, the flowers becoming not only finer but of a deeper purple and serving for fresh and dried arrangements alike.

That discovery, and others, made her more than ever observant of her world. Searching for wild plants that might prove grist to her mill was like building a bridge back across the years to a scene long past. Tidewater Virginia became for her, as for Mark Catesby and his contemporaries, full of "spontaneous Flowers."

The Williamsburg practice is to use the everlastings only during the three winter months. Dried bouquets are also supplemented—freshened—by displays of potted plants and evergreens: pine, cedar, bayberry, southern magnolia, and holly. (You will find in Chapter VIII some notes on the harvesting, drying, and handling of plants used for dry arrangements, along with a list of the mainstays used in Williamsburg.)

◀ 26. This summertime harvest in the drying room includes baptisia and goldenrain tree pods, pink and red celosia, strawflowers, yellow yarrow, goldenrod, honesty, marigolds, and teazel.

V

A Legacy of Containers

N OW, CONTAINERS! You may see a splendid array of them in restored Williamsburg among the superb collection of eighteenth-century ceramics. There are containers of pewter, glass, and brass, even of wood—"treen" in old England—but for the most part the vases and bowls and "bricks" are of pottery and porcelain. The Williamsburg collection of delft is one of America's finest, and surely Louise Fisher's call for authentic old containers spurred on the building of it.

Dutch William and his English princess and queen, Mary II, made the English royal family a mixture of both origin and sovereignty that, as we shall see, was repeated in the origin and spreading popularity of delft. History sums up Mary as a homebody whose enthusiasms were her gardens, her church, and helping the poor. She was, it is true, far from being an imperious Elizabeth I, yet Mary's influence today is wide and growing, while the great Elizabeth—whom we see in the portrait in the Capitol—lives only in books, chiefly as the Gloriana for whom the gallant Raleigh spread his cloak upon the mud.

◀ 27. Gardening in all its branches stretched
green fingers into a multitude of trades.
Pottery was designed specifically for the display
of flowers, as was this English delft urn
overflowing with irises and tulips.

65

Homebody Mary was twenty-six years old when she became mistress of Hampton Court and its gardens. As we have seen, she collected exotics. She reenters our scene with the reputation, vouched for by historians, of England's first flower "arranger," one who insisted upon, and got, ceramics designed especially for her bouquets.

I doubt if Mrs. Fisher, in rounding up examples of the amazing progeny that stemmed from Mary's innovations, ever saw any parallel of her own work with the queen's. But I do. Both knew their flowers by growing them; both were pioneers, Mary as the introducer of a new trend out of which would grow an industry, Mrs. Fisher as the reviver of that trend and its industry. Moreover, each woman was accustomed to showing off her bouquets in a rare vase or bowl in a palace—Hampton Court for Queen Mary, the governor's mansion for Mrs. Fisher.

Their final common bond was that neither woman had recourse to putty, string, wire, weighted spikes, and the like, which most modern arrangers regard as musts. No evidence of their use during Williamsburg's heyday could be found, much to Mrs. Fisher's own pleasure. She confessed to me that she simply did not have the termperament to work with them. She did find, however, and put to use a heavy crisscross square flower holder to keep flowers in place while fixing the basic outline for a shallow bowl bouquet; and she found, too, that the early potters—by request—had designed ingenious built-in supports in some of the old "posy holders."

Until Queen Mary's time, recorded instances are few indeed of containers being used in England exclusively for displaying flowers, and those few were pots. The inventory of the contents of a country house in 1556 lists a "blewe potte [glass] for flowers" valued at one penny; and in 1613 an account of the Maske of Flowers performed at Whitehall on Twelfth Night tells of the "great pottes of gilliflowers [carnations] which shadowed certaine lights placed behind them." Other than pots, containers were ordinarily some bowl or dish about the house, such as the bottle-shaped ewers and pitchers in daily use. These, for example, might have been of glass or of a tin-enameled earthenware.

About 1600, the tin-enameled industry was centered at Delft, Holland, and its products subsequently became known as delft or delftware. By mid-century, following the development of new techniques in painting and finishing this ware, Delft became the hub of the ceramic industry in northern Europe. Leading Delft potters about this

▶

28. Eighteenth-century English flower containers in the Colonial Williamsburg Collection. With the exception of a Worcester vase, the top two shelves contain pieces of English delft. On the third shelf are saltglaze vases, Worcester and Chelsea porcelains, and a pair of Chinese export porcelain vases. The fourth shelf holds English delft containers and two Staffordshire earthenware vases.

time were also influenced by oriental porcelain imported by the Dutch East India Company and reflected its designs in their products. In addition, the designers of Dutch delft borrowed from Persia, so it is believed, the idea of vases for bulb growing. These, used for tulips and hyacinths, were made with a number of upward pointing spouts to hold the growing bulbs whose roots trailed down to water inside the vessel. Also, there was the "pagoda"—a series of separate water trays superimposed one upon another. Delftware could be had in polychrome, but it was the fresh color theme of Chinese "blue and white" porcelain that caught the eye of the Dutch decorators and the fancy of the western world—and Queen Mary. She, according to Defoe, was so entranced by this style that she introduced into England the custom of decorating rooms with what today we loosely call "chinaware."

Pending the completion of new state apartments at Hampton Court, the young queen lived in the Water Gallery, formerly used as a landing place from the River Thames but now a royal household. Here, waiting for riverboats that plied up the Thames, she anticipated her imported luxuries just as eagerly as the Virginia plantation owner who stood on his wharf and gazed down the James for the appearance of a sail.

Sir Christopher Wren refurbished the Water Gallery for Mary as "the pleasantest little thing within doors that could possibly be made, with all the little neat curious things that suited her convenience." Ceilings and panels were painted, and Grinling Gibbons festooned doorways and cornices with his rich carvings of fruit and flowers. Chimneypieces were designed with stepped up diminishing shelves. upon which Mary placed her ceramics, and a master cabinetmaker was called in to erect cabinets in "the Delft-Ware Closett." Close by the Water Gallery was a dairy, a cool stone-floored room in which the butter was churned and the milk and eggs kept. I can well imagine that the dairy must have proved a perfect place for Her Majesty to arrange her flowers. So much delight did she take in the dairy that she had the potters design special milk pans of delft, which are now priceless.

Meanwhile, potters located for the most part on the south bank of the Thames in London began to produce tin-enameled earthenware. From there, manufacture of the ware spread to Bristol and Liverpool and became so closely related to the delftware of Delft that the average purchaser could hardly determine whether a piece had been made in England or in Holland.

Queen Anne, upon taking the throne, pursued her sister Mary's fondness for ceramics. Under the royal leadership, "chinaware" for

29. The pierced top of a square reproduction delft brick, and
a similar brick containing a mixed bouquet of snapdragons,
China asters, tansy, celosia, marigold, and coreopsis.

house decoration became a universal passion among the well-to-do and gradually supplanted pewter and "treen" in everyday household use. There were also practical reasons for the increasing use of ceramics. The Dutch and English East India Companies that had introduced China's porcelain had likewise introduced the dried leaves of a plant that was to prove as lucrative as tobacco. Tea (pronounced *tay*), by the end of the seventeenth century, had become a fashionable drink. And imitation of the Chinese manner of serving it, in drinking vessels that were both elegant and resistant to heat, created a demand that was supplied by the newer wares.

The rise of town life anticipated a broadening use of containers. As Thomas Fairchild, the London nurseryman for whom Catesby worked, put it:

> I find that most persons whose business requires them to be constantly in town, will have something of a garden at any rate. One may guess the general love my fellow citizens have of gardening, in furnishing their rooms and chambers with basons of flowers and Bough pots, rather than not have something of a garden before them.

The cut-flower trade began, and the potters who had sought to please a queen by designing delft containers to her liking rose to meet a popular demand for them that grew apace with town and city life. As always, competition engendered new ideas, fresh venturing, and improved quality, to the extreme of an amusing turnabout. The potters of old Cathay, who had been the imitated, now began imitating the new wares of English and European potters, even to decorating their porcelain with European flowers and producing personal designs specified by the Dutch and English East India Companies.

As a collector of our own day, Mrs. Fisher enjoyed an advantage that Queen Mary, who had merely begun the boom, might have envied. The queen was limited to Chinese export porcelain, to delftware containers of her own suggesting, and to other containers then available. Mrs. Fisher could draw upon much of the varied abundance and artistry of the succeeding eighteenth century—an output, from a flower arranger's viewpoint, unequalled since.

To the "basons" and "Bough pots" in which young Queen Mary had placed her flowers was added the wide range of containers that one may see and marvel over in the Williamsburg collection. It includes vases and jardinieres, pots with and without saucers, wall pockets plain

▶

30. An extremely rare four-tiered Bristol-made delft vase with snippets of Queen Anne's lace, calendula, yellow French marigold, tansy, nigella, yellow and pink celosia, mint, globe amaranth, feverfew, and golden marguerite.

and fancy—some shaped as cornucopias and known as "flower horns." To me, most practical and attractive among the innovations for one wishing to relive the period with flowers, are the quite small round, square, oblong, or triangular "bricks" with ingenious holes and openings at the top to hold the flowers in place. Tureens, pitchers, and punch bowls no doubt also served a dual purpose. Ceramic, silver, silver-gilt, pewter, and brass bowls with scalloped edges to support inverted wine glasses for cooling are called monteiths—after, the story goes, a "fantastical Scot" by that name who "wore the bottome of his cloake or coate so notched."

Coincidental to delft's growing versatility in the seventeenth century, gray salt-glazed stoneware found its way from Germany into England. There Staffordshire potters improved on it, creating a thin white ware. These refinements in the manufacture and salt-glazing of porcelain led to the replacement of delft on the English dinner table. By mid-century the products of Chelsea, Bow, Worcester, Derby, and other porcelain manufacturers had achieved worldwide acceptance. In the latter half of the 1700s saltglaze in turn was supplanted by the development in the Staffordshire potteries of an earthenware refined by one of the century's master potters and called "cream-coloured" and "Queensware."

The potter's name was Josiah Wedgwood. A farsighted, efficient businessman, Wedgwood was as much a promoter of his wares as he was a practicing craftsman. And he was outstanding among his contemporaries in the range of his products. His series of variously contrived flower holders is not only an indication of the prevailing national interest in flowers as part of the interior decoration of the home, but also of his own family's horticultural interests. A son, you may remember, was the founder of the Royal Horticultural Society of London, and one of his daughters became the mother of the great English naturalist, Charles Darwin.

In considering designs for bough pots, flower and root containers of all kinds, promoter Wedgwood took the trouble to find out from friends and customers which styles they most preferred. To his partner, Thomas Bentley, he wrote in 1772 that some of his patrons "prefer these things with the spouts much as the old Delph ones, they say that sort keep the flowers distinct and clever." And further, "Vases are furniture for a chimney-piece [mantel], bough pots for a hearth. . . . I think they can never be used one instead of another."

Famous for his Wedgwood creamware, in the flower arranger's interest he perforated, festooned, or enameled it. He also produced a variety of other wares such as cane-colored ware, black basalt with reliefs in red, and jasper ware in all its range. He made "bouquetiers of red and white biscuit," "myrtle pans of cane-leaf pattern," "flower jars purple and green enameled," and "bulbous root-pots in pebble and gold." There were also Wedgwood "dice-worked flower pots at one shilling," and "blue-ground flower pots with griffin heads and laurel festoons, eight inches high, at fifteen shillings each."

The times, prices, and names have changed: pots and jars and posy holders have become containers, a name that might puzzle Queen Mary and old Josiah if they should visit restored Williamsburg. I'm sure, however, that both would feel very much at home there, viewing familiar things each lent a hand in creating, and that Josiah especially, with his keen business sense, would be elated by this unique resurgence. Visitors to Williamsburg may now own a faithful reproduction of many eighteenth-century flower holders. Some of them, still produced by the firm that bears his name, are just like Josiah himself made them. For that rare anachronism, full credit is due to Louise Fisher for her twenty-three years of bringing down yesterday's bouquets from the attic of history.

VI

Painting with Flowers

Y EAR IN AND YEAR OUT, Colonial
Williamsburg's old-time bouquets are
probably seen by more people than any
other flower arrangements in America.
Among the questions visitors ask most often are
what are the flowers, and who arranges them.
At the time this book was written, Miss Edna S.
Pennell, who has now retired, was responsible for
the flower arrangements, and she allowed me to
accompany her on her rounds.

One June day, just a step behind Edna Pennell
as she chose and cut and fixed her day's round
of bouquets, I made it my task to learn precisely
her calendar of duties. It is a full calendar. The
first order of her day, six days a week through
March until the end of November, is the gathering and arranging of fresh flowers for the Governor's Palace and for the George Wythe and
Brush-Everard houses, both close by, fronting on
Palace Green. Also, during June through November, she must harvest her everlastings and
wild plants and see to their drying. The dried
arrangements are made and set in place toward
the end of November to serve through the winter

◀ 31. Textiles and embroideries followed the floral
theme. These bedhangings of white linen
embroidered with polychrome crewel yarn are
usually to be seen in a bedchamber in the
Wythe House during the summer months.

75

until March again provides fresh blooms, but they don't serve without green company. Supplementing them with evergreens from gardens and woods is a task that never lets up throughout the winter. And all year round the épergnes on dining room tables must be kept freshly supplied and dressed with fruits, sweetmeats, and nuts of the season.

No especial decorating is done for Thanksgiving. Although festivals were observed to celebrate the harvest, in colonial Virginia Thanksgiving Day was not, like today, a fixed holiday. Therefore much of late November goes into preparing both indoor and outdoor decorations for Christmastime, which is observed from Christmas Eve until January 6—Twelfth Night, or, as some call it, Candlemas Eve. On that day the old custom or superstition decreed that the adornments should come down.

"As you know," said Miss Pennell, beginning to describe her work, "there is a tendency to refer to 'Williamsburg arrangements.' I'd much rather have them described as eighteenth-century arrangements in their proper colonial setting, because that is what they really are—not arrangements created by Colonial Williamsburg any more than we created the architectural style of our colonial buildings." Of course, she made clear, both her flower and fruit arrangements are her own interpretations, just as those in the eighteenth-century household represented the taste of the colonial housewife; and this will continue to hold for whoever carries on the work in the future. Yet, the guides provided by research—the flowers, the containers, the settings—will always remain the same.

Style, Miss Pennell explained, is a product of individual taste. If one has an eye for style, one will see that the way each person arranges her flowers is as revealing of her personality as her handwriting or the tone of letters she writes or the cut of her coat.

"Provided," I suggested, "that she is not bound by iron rules and merely copies what's in the book."

"As far as we know, there were no rules for bouquet-making in the old days," she replied. "Women through the ages have picked and brought flowers into their homes because they loved them and loved to arrange them as prettily as they could, as they would the colored threads in a piece of needlework. It is both an artistic and creative expression that all women have in some measure, and women almost instinctively like to beautify their homes.

"And all the evidence indicates that the average eighteenth-century housewife wanted to show off her flowers rather than display her skill

32. A close-up of an arrangement of coreopsis, calendula, and field daisies in a vase of English saltglaze, with the figure of a cat in salt-glazed agate beside it.

in arranging them. At a time when interest in plant exploration and botany ran high, people would surely have on occasion been proud of a single bloom and would have brought it indoors to display it. That is why, now and then, I place one choice bloom on a window sill or in the Governor's study."

"Did women in the old days pattern their bouquet-making after the painted flower pieces of Dutch and Flemish artists?" I asked. It may be, she conceded, that among a favored few some tried to reproduce the artists' work, although there is no record that anyone did. Even then, she reminded me, the flower painters rarely copied another's work but intuitively followed the principles of composition that every good artist or designer or craftsman learns in time to follow: scale, harmony, balance, and design. Those principles are the same in all creative work.

Miss Pennell said that she herself has studied the old Dutch flower paintings in detail, because she thinks of her work as painting with flowers and, like the artist's, being guided by the tried principles of all good composition. As for those of us who may try to pattern our own arranging after hers, it is comforting to know that people generally prefer not the grand but the smaller, simpler bouquets that, Miss Pennell grants, anyone may enjoy doing.

She summed up the principles of her bouquet-making as follows:

1. The size, or *scale,* of the finished arrangement is determined by the space it will occupy. The size of the container determines the overall size of the arrangement.
2. *Harmony* can only be achieved by keeping in mind the colors of the walls, the floor covering, curtains, and upholstery. Both flowers and container should blend with the furnishings and become part of the overall decoration of the room.
3. In a mass arrangement of different kinds of flowers, typical of the colonial period, the *design* is often a fan-shaped outline. *Balance,* line, and a center of interest may be achieved both through color and through contrast of form and texture in plant material.

It was six o'clock on a typical June morning in Williamsburg when I drove out with her to the cutting garden. It had rained during the night and was still raining off and on as the flower picking began. Luckily the blooms were not too sodden. Up and down the rows we went, gathering armfuls of larkspurs, Oriental poppies, and thermopsis with its long, lupine-like spikes of yellow blooms. (That poppy—*Papaver orientale*—was introduced into England from Armenia in 1714, and at once Peter Collinson sent seeds to John Bartram.) Along the fence line there was a grouping of old shrubs and here we cut sprays of mock orange, elder-flower heads still in bud, and viburnum. "I'm glad these old shrubs were left here," Miss Pennell said. "Old shrubs are best for cutting, so they have a real use in gardens, though horticulturists like to replace them."

"Picking is one of the most important things in making flower arrangements; it adds to enjoyment and brings you down to earth," she volunteered, unperturbed by the wet. "You have to *know* your flowers, and you can truly know them only through contact with nature. You must get out in the rain, know flowers in all weather, all their life-times." On the way back we passed through some outlying areas where there were magnificent, tall, spreading southern magnolias *(M. grandiflora)*. With the long-handled pruner and with practiced dexterity, her driver-helper snipped off a bloom and caught it as it fell. If he had missed, the bloom would have been bruised and thus spoiled for the Palace bouquet it was scheduled to adorn. Two or three more such blooms were likewise secured and we went directly to the Palace.

The picking had been finished before eight o'clock. Straightaway the work of arranging began. Twelve or thirteen flower groups, some large, some small, are maintained in the Palace. Making them up may take from one to three hours, according to how many bouquets must be entirely remade. This day nine were to be made afresh, the others re-furbished. The day's materials happened to have come mainly from the cutting garden, and wildflowers and herbs were being planned as accents, although often the order is reversed, or again, as of old, garden flowers and wildflowers are blended equally. Sometimes wildflowers go into the pot alone. Any or all herbs may at times be seen in the bou-quets, including lavender and even chives. As to wildflowers—Miss Pennell reminded me—they are as well loved today as when the womenfolk of the colonial plantations, accompanying their husbands to Williamsburg for Assembly time, brought bunches of wildflowers for kin and friends in town.

Goldenrod, Queen Anne's lace, and sorrel are standbys in today's arrangements: goldenrod with sunflowers and Queen Anne's lace with sorrel. These are mixtures that always please visitors. Too, buttercups stand high among the public's old favorites; so does boneset, that cure-all of yesterday's ills when in every knowing farmhouse it was brewed into boneset tea.

The flower group on which Miss Pennell worked as she talked was destined for a side table against the putty-colored wall of the Palace dining room. Choosing a Chinese export porcelain bowl, she began to build her flower piece, working from back to front. I noted each step:

1. Branches of pine provided a green background.
2. Working from the center, and building sidewise in a fan pattern, spikes of yellow thermopsis completed the outline of the design.

3. Virburnum sprays and white and yellow Dutch iris, the yellow predominating, were used as fillers and so arranged as to create a third dimension, or depth.
4. Blood-red Oriental poppies were placed high and low near the center to provide an eye-catching thread of color and a center of interest.

Translated into today's flower arranging vocabulary, all this may read: use *primary plant material,* which is spiky and tapers to a point, for the outline of the design; use *secondary plant material,* often spoken of as filler—branching, graceful flowers and shrubs—in the center of the bouquet; and use *tertiary plant material,* round and weighty, to give a center of interest or to tie the design together.

Miss Pennell's running commentary drew attention to small but important details. "You don't have to stick your flowers straight in," she stressed while placing her fillers. "The horizontal line is important and you build up from it." And again, "Flowers are lovely in profile, and I like to see a flower head turning away from the viewer." "Buds are always effective," she said when I commented on a half-open poppy bud with a slash of brilliant red unfurling from the green hood. In pauses between moments of concentration she let fall some of her maxims. Essentially random remarks, I repeat them here because they reveal the sort of thinking that lies behind the work of her hands:

People often say, "I could do arrangements if, like you, I had a lot of containers." You don't need a lot. Pick one appropriate to your room, and the changing flowers give you a different picture throughout the year.

Flower arranging can be enjoyed even if you aren't naturally artistic. You don't have to be an expert to get pleasure from it.

You remember Fleming Brown, the old major-domo at the Palace? He was such a nice person. I often heard him say to those who worked with him, "Fair won't do, it's got to be perfect." I like that advice.

I always remember what Charles Eliot, president of Harvard, also said of landscape architecture, "What would be fair must first be fit." That applies to flower arranging too. To please, an arrangement must fit into its surroundings in color, proportion, and style. Flower arrangements are part of the interior decoration.

A good design must be alive, display contrasts. Contrast gives vitality—the gradations we see in nature, light to dark, seed to fruit, morning to night.

▶

33. Red bergamot, or bee-balm, among a predominantly green bouquet of herbs set in a slipware pot in the Wythe House kitchen. The herbs include tansy, clary sage, common sage, coriander, oregano, borage, and rue. Parsley and lemon thyme lie on the table.

As she talked, my thoughts wandered back to the familiar scenes of my previous visit to Williamsburg, and I recalled the times I'd fished for crabs along Indian Creek and in the James River for whatever came to my bait, mostly catfish. So thinking, a maxim came to mind that Izaak Walton had laid down for angling, one that it seemed Miss Pennell might like to add to her list. Angling, said Walton, is

> somewhat like poetry; men are to be born so, I mean with inclinations to it, though both may be heightened by discourse and practice; but he that hopes to be a good angler must not only bring an inquiring, searching, observing wit, but . . . a love and propensity to the art itself.

My favorite among the things done that day was a loose and informal bouquet of mock orange arranged in one of the old square bricks. It looked so pretty and fresh and free. Pleased, Miss Pennell commented, "People are so inclined to stick stems straight up in these old flower holders, though the stems are supported just as well if slipped in sideways on the horizontal plane. Do that, and they droop into their natural curves." She added, "I sometimes use two kinds of flowers, or more, in the bricks, but I like them as well with flowers of one kind. A brick is ideal for sweet peas and daffodils."

"I love color, and I love that of poppies and nasturtiums especially," she said. "They echo the richness of the old flower prints and tie in with the brocades and other rich furnishings in the Palace rooms."

The nasturtium came to England from Peru around 1596, probably brought by some Elizabethan seadog who had raided a homeward-bound Spanish galleon. It became highly esteemed for its flowers, tender leaves, and seeds or "capuchin capers." The flowers and leaves were used in salads, the capers pickled and "used in stewings all winter." John Randolph of Williamsburg, in *A Treatise on Gardening*, wrote, "It is thought the flower is superior to a radish in flavour, and is eat in salads, or without." And Thomas Jefferson planted "Nasturtium in 35 little hills" at Monticello.

Into a small pewter bowl, for her last bouquet of the morning, Miss Pennell tucked a little fluffy cluster of pansies, sweet William, veronica, thyme, and feverfew. The last, a hardy perennial border plant, is a wonderful "filler" and, like the herbs, is one of the most useful plants to have on hand in good supply. She stood back and eyed this diminutive array. "Almost everybody likes a little thing," she said as she dried her hands.

It was later than usual, probably because of my own interruptions, and the Palace was already thronged with visitors. We threaded our way from room to room to see that every arrangement was in its appointed place and that fallen petals had been swept up.

Over an early lunch Miss Pennell offered to take the next morning off and go with me through the exhibition buildings, room by room, before they were open to the public. Alone, I had already made those rounds many times, each time noticing some detail that I had previously missed, for every room is full of memories and treasures. For me, the next day was to add even more to them.

VII

Bouquets for A Williamsburg Setting

THIS JUNE MORNING promised a day of sunshine. The early light and the warmth rapidly dried the dew that overnight had freshened Colonial Williamsburg's one hundred acres of gardens and greens. Sometimes I think it is only the mockingbirds who know Williamsburg at its best—at dawn, when only they are yet astir and can see brightening against a pink sky the sharp, trim roof lines of the old houses.

Eighty-eight buildings of the eighteenth and early nineteenth centuries still remain in and near the Historic Area; counted among the others that have been reconstructed on their original sites are a few of the public buildings, many residences, and scores of outbuildings that fell victim to fire and deterioration before the Restoration began. The Palace and the Capitol were among those burned to the ground.

I knew that flower arrangements were used in all the exhibition buildings that had been homes. In answer to my question Edna Pennell said, "It isn't likely that flowers were used in buildings

◀ 34. Tea time in the main bedchamber, Peyton Randolph House, with a Chelsea tea service; a tea kettle, china on copper, is from Canton. The chair is upholstered in brocaded wool damask. Poppy anemones and species tulips are set in a Chinese vase.

85

such as the Capitol." "They were household ornaments, and so we place them in what were the town's most outstanding households."

"As essential, say, as mirrors?"

"I think so, indeed I do. Things like looking glasses and tables and chairs are unchanging and lifeless. Flowers bring renewed freshness and color into a room, give it a feeling of being lived in."

Visitors to Colonial Williamsburg—naturally the women, but also an astonishing number of men and children—seem to agree with Miss Pennell. The flower arrangements inspire as many questions as any other detail of the decor of the Palace or its neighbors. A letter, so typical of many in the Flower Section's mailbag, bears this out: "I just wanted to say the flowers make things seem alive; they show that someone has been in the room who cared about it and thought about it."

Edna Pennell does care. She told me, "If you live here and soak up the atmosphere of colonial days, you inevitably come to express it in whatever you create." Many a time, as she picks her wildflowers, she wonders if the same flower grew in the same place years ago, for just outside Williamsburg much is pasture still; and she often fancies, placing her bouquets, that she may be putting the same flowers in the same spot in a room as did some colonial dame long before her. Too, she has a love of chinaware for its own sake, as did the queens, Mary and Anne. I could tell this in the way she handled two favorite containers that she wanted me to see before we set out on our round. One was a crocus pot in Worcester procelain decorated with floral sprays and butterflies in blue—ideal for a bedside table. The other was a small pyramid-shaped French delft-style flower holder, the attached cone top pierced with holes just right for short-stemmed flowers.

While cutting and arranging, Miss Pennell thinks constantly about the detail of the rooms so that the flowers will be placed in the most pleasing relation to their environment. She explained, as we walked along the Palace Green, that a room with dark walls calls for white, yellow, and orange flowers, for light and yellow greens, while reds and purples make good additions where light falls on the bouquet. White, cream, and light green walls will take flowers of all colors, especially those of dark or strong hues. Not only the walls, but also the curtains and the furniture upholstery must be considered, for the bouquet should harmonize with its surroundings to be pleasing. There may be infinite contrast in flower color and foliage material, comparable to the variety of color stitched into wool needlework, but the whole should be in accord with the general scheme of the room. Colors are varied depending upon the season: bright flowers in spring, cool tints in summer, a crescendo of brilliance for autumn, and of course the need for bright blossoms during winter is met by the everlastings.

The heavy Palace doors were not yet open to the visitors, but the custodian admitted us as we continued to talk—now of placing arrangements to their best advantage. I gathered that their position within a room needs a knowing consideration that is directly tied in with a knowledge of the flowers. Many distinctive, stately flowers—the large bouquets of gladiolus, hollyhock, and foxglove—demand a background. They are best set on tables close by walls and, for safety, outside the main stream of traffic. Common sweet flowers such as daffodils, sweet peas, violets, and primroses—flowers that have attained a place of special affection out of tradition, abundance, and ease of cultivation— are best placed within reach. And all flowers will last longer if not set near open windows, in drafts, too close to fireplaces or heat outlets, or where the sun may strike.

The parlor, our first stop, is smallish as Palace rooms go, a room that I am sure would have delighted Queen Mary. She was an expert needlewoman and is said to have worked as hard at her craft as though she had to make her living by it. She would have appreciated the skill of hand evident in the small carpet on the parlor floor, and the English chair, with its brilliant flowers in wool needlework still as fresh as everlastings properly dried.

Arrayed along the chimneypiece, similar to those listed in the inventory of a royal governor, are eleven Chelsea porcelain figures of birds (so scarce that the group was not completed until 1961). Other choice ceramic examples include a pyramidal delft vase. Looking down on us from her portrait above the chimneypiece was a young lady. She had sat for the painting with flowers in her hair and flowers around the straw hat in her lap. In the top left-hand corner of the painting I noticed a cardinal perched on the branch of a tree. As still there as the porcelain birds on the mantel, in real life the cardinal is Virginia's state bird.

On a side table, just inside the door, Miss Pennell had placed her flowers; they are usually arranged in a small blue and white delft urn, one of her favorite and most useful containers. I have seen this urn displaying dianthus, feverfew, larkspur, blue veronica, cornflowers (blue, deep blue, and pink); and later in the season, lavender, bergamot, gaillardia, and coreopsis, picking up the colors in the parlor's needlepoint and china.

Aside from the family quarters of the governor, the rooms of the Palace are spacious and ornate. The same words are descriptive of their flower arrangements, which I saw—as Miss Pennell so painstakingly had intended them to be—as bouquets of state. I had watched her make those massive displays of many flowers in large containers and was well aware that it was her most difficult task. Formality and the dazzling elegance of Assembly balls ruled the stately mass arrangements in the ballroom. Today the bouquets contained the flowers described in yesterday's picking, but I also remembered others that stay in mind as especially lovely for this room: mixed bouquets of mock orange, deep red peony, and sweet William, or of lilac, or of mountain laurel.

Upstairs, in the "great bedchamber," I admired a delft brick overflowing with mock orange and poppies, carmine to rose pink, that added a touch of lightness to the ornately carved walnut four-poster bed. Sweet William and veronica, picking up the colors of crewelwork bed hangings in the adjoining bedroom, adorned the small alcove that connects the two. The large family sitting room known as the "upper middle room"—with dark woodwork and dark, tooled leather wall hangings—calls for bold flowers and foliage. Goldenrod and sunflowers are often used here in late summer, but this day there was an armful of the Southern magnolia on a center table. Not only was this magnolia hailed in England as "the most elegant tree that has ever been introduced into Europe," but in Williamsburg it may also be described as the flower arranger's most useful evergreen. The great lemon-scented white blooms can be used in June, the scarlet studded seed cones in September and October. As for the shining foliage, this is a staple throughout the year.

We came at length to the governor's study, which sits just off the broad upstairs hallway. There on a side table sat a small seven-inch-high Chinese porcelain vase trailing sprays of coral honeysuckle—the native vine that grew all over William Byrd's summerhouse at Westover and that Jefferson also liked so well. This simple arrangement struck just the right note for the end of the Palace tour and our going from the official residence of royal governors to the more modest George Wythe House nearby.

The restored Wythe House is a world removed from the Palace, a haven for intimate living, a home of charm and good taste. Here lived scholarly George Wythe, who instructed Thomas Jefferson in law and remained his "most affectionate friend through life." Here Jefferson

35. Painting with flowers. Species tulips, anemones, narcissus,
scilla, and lilac fill a Derby porcelain bowl set on a dressing
table in the Peyton Randolph House. The soap box beside it is
of enamel on copper, with gilt metal mounts.

and his family stayed for several weeks in historic 1776. Later, the
house served as Washington's personal headquarters before the Battle
of Yorktown.

It is hard to say which of the first floor rooms delighted me most:
the study, enhanced with a striking portrait of George Washington,
attributed to Gilbert Stuart, or the parlor with its old books in leather
bindings, or the dining room with its china cupboard. White walled,
with olive green woodwork, all three are light rooms with pleasant
vistas of the out-of-doors. The same decor applies throughout the
house.

The Wythe dining room shows off bowls and épergnes of fruit to unusual advantage. Pineapples and lemons pick up the rare yellow gold

shade of the curtains and chair seats, a shade that is repeated in the painted back of the corner cupboard. The setting is superb for smooth-skinned nectarines, velvet-skinned peaches, cherries, plums, figs, red currants, and, above all, for the warm flush of the freckled apricot.

On the way upstairs in the Wythe House you cannot fail to notice the original prints from Robert Furber's *Twelve Months of Flowers* on the staircase wall. These illustrations are valuable guides to the plants available during the Georgian period, for they show the flowers of each season throughout the year, arranged in colorful mass bouquets.

Do not, however, let Furber's prints entirely distract you from "Earth," a small print in the Wythe upstairs hall. The picture was painted in green, red, and brown for one Robert Sayer, Fleet Street, London, and inscribed:

> As the sweet Flower from Earth delightfull springs
> And rivals in its Pomp the Pride of Kings,
> So the bright Maid not deck'd with Pride or Birth
> An Angel seems and makes a Heaven of Earth

If ever I had been a guest in the Wythe House I would have been happiest to have occupied the northwest bedroom on the garden side, although my choice was almost a tossup among the four bedrooms. That facing Palace Green would be fun—to watch the passers-by going to and from the Palace and to look across the Green through Catesby's catalpa trees. There is a fine four-poster bed with antique rose pink hangings that match the room's window curtains, and a handy round bedside table upon which sits always a bunch of flowers, also of the period.

But the garden-view bedroom at the other end of the landing wins, for me, by a short margin. It has a most delectable looking "field bed," so called because its top suggests a tent—a light canopy frame, covered with white muslin, gracefully arched over slender supporting posts. Compare this simple bedstead, made late in the eighteenth century, with the far older, heavily carved four-poster in the great bedchamber of the Palace, and you will see, through the medium of bedsteads, what happened in the colonial period's changeover from formal to informal gardens, from dark-paneled to light, painted walls, from heavy earthenware pottery to blue and white delft, and from delft to the English saltglaze and porcelain of Wedgwood and others.

This Wythe bedroom provides one of the most beautiful vignette views in all Williamsburg, across George Wythe's miniature "plantation" garden with its hedge of fig trees and well-ordered, comprehensive herb garden flanking flower beds planted frankly for enjoyment. On the broad, deep window seat there may be a bouquet, as surely there must have been when Jefferson and others were guests. This day the flowers were larkspurs, veronica, and pink and blue cornflowers. It is essentially a room for light, delicately colored blooms. In spring, for instance, apple blossoms, pink tulips, and lilac, separately or all together, have their turn.

The Wythe House saw a lot of the town life of eighteenth-century Williamsburg; yet opposite it across the Palace Green, the Brush-Everard House saw even more—through eyes as varied in outlook as those of the original builder, gunsmith John Brush, and William Dering, an early occupant who was an artist and dancing master. Others lived there continuously for more than 240 years, until 1946. It was the small white house of Mary Johnston's novel *Audrey,* published in 1902 after her enormously popular story of old Virginia, *To Have and to Hold.* For me, no other house in Williamsburg so well reflects the changing tastes of our ancestors.

Gardening plainly was a favorite recreation for Thomas Everard, the mayor of Williamsburg who bought this property along about mid-century, for his old home is the only one in the restored capital that can boast a garden toolhouse. It was probably he who planted the dwarf boxwood that has now grown into gnarled "trees" along the central walk of the formal garden—the oldest box in Williamsburg. It is also believed that Everard created the informal or natural garden close by, where wandering serpentine walks lead to what was a little pond or dam, now dry, snuggling in the small ravine. This was a break with tradition then most daring in formal Williamsburg, and no doubt was much debated.

I imagine that of all the owners of this antique place, Thomas Everard would be the one most pleased to see his prim little home tastefully spotted here and there with flowers that enhance the furnishings, without themselves becoming display pieces. I made special note of the medley of blooms in the library: a bouquet of yellow day lilies arranged in an old Chinese cachepot in company with orange butterfly weed, yellow yarrow, coreopsis, and wild black-eyed Susans. I noted the harmony of this flower piece with its setting: the yellow flowers echoed the yellow-flowered wallpaper that had been reproduced from the remains of colonial wallpaper found in the house; the eyes of the

36. This superb container, Chinese export porcelain, is brimming over with red bergamot, snapdragons white and red, gladioli, coreopsis, oak-leaved hydrangea, and day lily. Chinese wallpaper in the Governor's Palace supper room provides the background.

black-eyed Susans picked up the black of the black-coated gentleman, one Jacob Fox, whose portrait by William Williams hangs on the wall.

The Brush-Everard library contains a very special collection of old books. In assembling it, researchers followed Thomas Jefferson's list of books that a gentleman's library or "study of books" should contain. There are, in all, 148 titles, among them Philip Miller's *Gardener's dict.*

Upstairs, by way of finely turned balusters and sweeping hand rails, a chimneypiece in one of the bedrooms is reserved for potted plants in season, in accord with the sage advice that "a Chimney thus done doth grace a Room exceedingly."

Of course, a gardener myself, I simply had to see the unique tool-house of the Brush-Everard garden, and there I found what to me were glories of old: the array of spades and hoes and rakes that any gardener's ghost of old Virginia would know at once. There were, besides, a mighty copper watering can that, full, only a man could heft, and a fine pair of weighing scales fashioned of wrought iron, with copper measuring pans. But it was the bell glass that enamored me most. A bell glass is a miniature, portable hothouse about the size and shape of an old-fashioned beehive. I recalled that Peter Kalm, the Swedish naturalist, had noticed the use of such glasses for forcing vegetables in the nursery gardens around London—five cauliflower plants to each glass. What's more, I remembered a bell glass that was always on hand in the garden of the Queen Anne house where I had spent my own early growing up.

Our bell glass was kept safely stowed away in a garden toolhouse much like Thomas Everard's and brought forth each December. Then the glass was placed over a clump of Christmas roses, both to hurry their blooming and to protect their white blooms from being spattered by rain and mud. I wondered if Thomas Everard had used his bell glass to like purpose for the Christmas of 1766, when he was mayor of Williamsburg. If there was meaning, not merely coincidence, in one of the old flower prints displayed in the Brush-Everard garden house he most certainly did, for the print is of several species of the Christmas rose.

VIII

Dry Arrangements for Winter

PROPERLY, everlastings are plants whose chaffy or papery flower parts hold their color when thoroughly dry. In today's revival of the use of dried flowers for winter decoration a vast range of either wild and cultivated flowers are used, as are ferns and grasses, corn tassels, wheat and barley ears, and leaves.

The first essential is a proper drying room. Like fine wines, the everlastings become that only when allowed to mature in isolation and darkness. To preserve their colors, the room must be kept dark, and to fit its purpose, bone-dry. A temperature a shade warmer than that of the outdoors should be maintained.

In Williamsburg, an attic room over one of the kitchens ideally supplies this all-important need. There the small windows are covered with black cloth and paper. Wires are strung from wall to wall, and from them, immediately after being gathered, hang each tied bunch of fresh blooms or foliage or seed heads or pods.

For a good harvest of everlastings, the mate-

◀ 37. A bouquet of dried flowers to lighten a dark winter's day is made up of honesty, bittersweet, strawflowers, Christmas fern, white yarrow, and Chinese lanterns in a German stoneware water jug.

95

rial must be gathered during all the six months from June through October. Many plants bloom intermittently through the summer and autumn until frost, so that no definite time can be fixed for their reaping. One compensation for this long season of collecting is that the blooms may be used at any time for fresh cut-flower arrangement, although once so used they should never be dried.

Harvesting at the right moment is as important as having an adequate drying room. Everyone learns by trial, failure, and that persistent teacher, experience, when that right moment is. The proper time is finally determined by a kind of sixth sense; and it varies according to the season and the climate in every locality.

Generally, the proper time for gathering is just before the plants have reached their prime, usually in the first flush of their bloom. Some plants, like goldenrod and other flowers that "fluff up," should be picked at an even earlier stage: when the buds are full and about to open. When so gathered, the process of flowering seems to continue after the bunches are hung up for drying. The blooms then fluff up, yet remain so securely compact afterward that they do not shatter when handled for arrangement.

To this may be added the caution that material picked after a hard rain will not dry successfully and that there are exceptions to the general rule of gathering when prime. Strawflowers and pearly everlastings, for example, are best when picked in the advanced bud stage.

After gathering, the stems of all flowers should be stripped of foliage and be tied in small bunches, about six to eight pieces to a bunch, and be hung upside down. Wilted material should be ruthlessly discarded.

Leaves should be gathered at the height of their fall color when still full of sap. If cut too late the leaves, when you come to use them, will flutter to the floor as you lift the branches. However, some leaves, such as beech, may be gathered still green. The green leaves give variety of contrasting effects.

In gathering the leaves, care must be taken to choose only those branches that are perfectly flat. So necessary is it to avoid wilting that it is well to place them immediately into a pail of water, and bring them thus into the drying room. There the leaves are placed on the floor for trimming and, this done, placed between papers where they should lie perfectly flat, with no two leaves overlapping. A number of layers of leaves may be piled one on the other, but it is essential that paper separate each layer. Finally, heavy boards are placed on top of the pile.

▶

38. A bouquet of dried flowers beneath the portrait
of an unknown gentleman brightens the hallway
of the Peyton Randolph House. The flowers are
red celosia, yellow strawflowers, cattails,
tansy, blue larkspur, and beech leaves.

The leaves will be ready to use in about three weeks, but unless they are entirely dry they will curl.

Ferns should be treated in the same way.

Weather conditions and the season determine somewhat the success of drying plant material. Thus, one variety may not be successful one year but will dry beautifully the next.

The handling of dried materials, once dried, should be limited to arranging them for final display, and as that is a messy affair it is best done in the drying room. Sand, as mentioned by Philip Miller—fine dry sand—gives a container the necessary weight, and is best for holding the stems in place.

Sand is the only aid used in the dried flower arrangements in Williamsburg. There is no known record of eighteenth-century use of modeling clay, florist's wire, paraffin wax, or borax.

However—another outgrowth of long experience—certain guidelines or principles are followed. In making the full-scale bouquets, the first step is to trace the outline with branches of dried leaves chosen to fit the scene in mind. Then, gradually, other materials in the required colors are used to fill in, working from the top down to the base. There the more solid flowers, the strawflowers, prince's plumes, and yarrow, are used in mass, with the lighter pearly everlastings and sea lavender above. White is used a good deal as a filler and to lighten the whole arrangement. To this end, quantities of boneset, pearly everlasting, and saltbush are effective. Generally speaking, white is used as the chief filler in making red-toned arrangements, goldenrod for the predominantly yellow ones.

Yellow beech leaves and green ferns, yellow strawflowers and red horse chestnut pods, yellow cockscomb and bittersweet make a fine array. So do maple leaves—in all their gamut of red and orange yellow—with yellow yarrow, artemisia, red prince's plume, cockscomb, and blazing star.

As I have already mentioned, the flowers and trees and shrubs in Williamsburg's Historic Area are restricted mostly to those known to eighteenth-century gardeners and plantsmen. This imposes a corresponding limitation on Colonial Williamsburg's flower arrangers.

Outside of Williamsburg, today's dried flower enthusiasts include in their arrangements an extraordinary range of plant material that might well have bemused colonial housewives. An entire industry has arisen in the last quarter of a century to meet the demand. Some dried flowers are shipped by air from such distant parts as Hawaii and

Brazil, packed tight to prevent shattering, in long cardboard boxes. The stems are wired, the flower heads dyed or sprayed in various colors. One of the chief growing areas for flowers destined for drying, and also one of the chief collecting and distributing centers for dried plant material, is near San Francisco.

I have an idea that Peter Collinson of London and John Custis of Williamsburg may have had a keener pleasure from the few everlastings at their disposal, such as the globe amaranth, than from the almost bewildering choice we have on hand today.

Some Plants for Winter Use

This is not intended as a comprehensive list of the wild and cultivated flowers, ferns and grasses, corn tassels, wheat and barley ears, and leaves that are adaptable for winter ornament. It does, however, include the basic material used by Colonial Williamsburg and the approximate times for harvesting in tidewater Virginia. The time for gathering, of course, varies widely in different climatic zones.

Cultivated Plants Grown in the Cutting Garden

Artemisia (gray foliage)	July—early
Baby's breath (white)	June
Baptisia pods (blue)	July, when pods have formed and turned blue
Bells of Ireland (green)	July
Bittersweet (vine)	Fall
Blue sage	September, as nights get cooler and color deepens
Celosia—cockscomb, plumed and crested (pink and red)	At maturity, from August onward
Chinese lanterns (orange)	September
Chives (mauve)	June
Fennel flower pods (reddish)	July—August
Feverfew (white)	July
Globe amaranth (white, pink, and magenta)	August until frost

Goldenrain tree pods (green)	Early July
Honesty (white)	August
Hydrangea (shrub)	July
Larkspur (pink, blue, and white)	June
Marigolds (yellow and orange)	Early September
Peony (red)	May
Rose hips (red)	August
Scarlet sage	August
Statice (white)	June
Strawflowers (all colors)	When buds develop. Pick in tight bud
Tansy (yellow)	August
Vitex (blue)	July
Yarrow (yellow and white)	Late June
Yorktown onion (lavender)	Early July

Wild Plants

Boneset	August
Butterfly weed (orange)	Late June
Cattails	July—early
Devil's walking stick (green)	Early August. Pick in bud
Dock (green and brown)	June
Goldenrod—the Canada, fragrant, plume, silver, wreath, and wrinkled varieties	August, early September. It is important that goldenrod be cut at the right time—when the buds are full and about to open
Grasses—broom-sedge, cloud, fox-tail, marram, plume, and spike varieties	Late May to fall
Pearly everlasting	September
Sumac	August
Wild mustard seed pods (wheat blond)	May

Leaves

Beech	June (if desired green) and several weeks during October—November
*Christmas fern	June
Maple, Norway	Last two weeks of October
Maple, sugar	Beginning of November
Poplar, white	June
*Royal fern	June
Sorrel	September

Other ferns have been discarded because of their tendency to curl and lose their shape. The royal and Christmas ferns retain their greenness.

IX

Knowing Your Flowers

H OW DO YOU MAKE your flowers last so well?" This is the question most often asked about the care of cut flowers.

The trick, if trick there be, lies in knowing the flowers, when to cut, and how to nurse them along while they are on display. In the old days there were no aspirin pills or other pellets for reviving cut flowers, and no such aids are used by Colonial Williamsburg's garden staff today.

Flowers, as all gardeners know, are generally in better condition in the very early morning than at any other time of the day, and that is when to gather them at their freshest and sweetest. Better while the dew is on their petals than after the dew has dried. The second best time to cut is in late evening; the worst is on clear summer days between eleven and three o'clock when the sun is highest. During early spring, late autumn, and winter, you need not be quite so particular, but Miss Pennell preferred in all seasons to cut her flowers in early morning.

Next in importance is to note the age of the flowers. Whenever possible, they should be cut

39. The Brush Everard garden house with its array of spades and hoes, its bell glass and copper watering can, displays—in somewhat casual fashion—flowers, vegetables, and fruits in season.

in bud, or when the bud is just about to open. This is their youth. Poppies and phlox, and iris particularly, repay this attention, as do many flowering shrubs and all fruit blossoms. Not only will the blooms last longer, but they will also yield more fragrance.

City dwellers who have no gardens must depend, as did many English townspeople in Philip Miller's day, upon the florist for their supplies. And many are the florists who feel they must offer flowers that are fully opened or at the peak of their beauty, and also their life. So the problem: when has a flower reached the age when its value as a cut flower is on the wane?

In the huge family of daisylike flowers such as asters or black-eyed Susans—known in its garden varieties as rudbeckias—the disk of florets in the center of each bloom will provide the answer. If all the florets have not opened and the disk retains a fresh, live color, it is still a good buy. No flowers last better than the composites, as these flowers are called, but if cut after they have attained their peak blooms they will not last any time at all.

With all blooms, as good a rule of thumb as any is to cut young. The young flowers usually retain some of the color of the bud, so look for it. You will, in time, come to notice that the yellows are slightly green in youth and are a deeper yellow, even orange tinted, in old age.

Flowers that bloom in clusters are at their best when the central bloom shows no sign of fading, at their worst when no unexpanded buds are to be found under the trusses of open blooms. In autumn, when frost seems likely next morning, cut in the evening the flowers that are not fully opened and they will keep fresh often for two or three weeks. If cut in bud, they may last a month or longer.

The lasting quality of *all* cut blooms depends upon the lapse of time between their cutting and being placed in water. Flowers that shed their petals quickly, poppies for example, are less inclined to do so if placed in water immediately after cutting. Wayside and field flowers are notably prone to droop—sometimes irrecoverably—if the immediate cut-to-water practice is not followed, a habit that has led many an arranger to reject them for lack of staying power. Gathered in the morning, immersed deeply and at once into water, they can last as long as many a garden flower.

To restore cut flowers that have flagged before they get their stems into water, nothing surpasses thrusting the stems deep into warm water—ninety degrees or so for soft-stemmed flowers, hotter for woody material. Hydrangeas and poppies, stripped of their lower foliage, may be plunged briefly into several inches of boiling water and then cooled off in a cold bath; or the cut stems may be singed in candle flame. Hollyhocks, if held in boiling water for about ten minutes and then transferred to a cold bath, will stay fresh four days. Queen Anne's lace, if allowed when first picked to remain six or eight hours in water in a cool, dark place, will stand erect when arranged. But no flower, however treated, ever equals in staying power the flower whose primitive freshness is not lost.

As to containers: they must be scrupulously clean if you would have their bouquets last. Soap lather with a little ammonia added is excellent for cleaning earthenware or metal; clean, rough sand for scouring glass.

For water, the best is rain or good well water, and tepid water is preferable to cold, which means that for city dwellers pure bottled water, rather than tap water, may be worth its cost especially if the tap water is heavily chlorinated.

In making the bouquet, stems should be stripped of all the lower leaves up to the point of immersion in water. Then, once the bouquet is placed on duty, keep in mind that fresh-cut flowers absorb much water the first day and that the container should be checked for needed refilling the next morning.

That brings us to the next question asked by so many puzzled visitors, "Why don't you ever use flowers on the dining room tables—always fruit?" I touched on this odd omission earlier, although I failed to tell then why colonial housewives preferred other than floral centerpieces. A practical reason probably dictated their preference, namely, the appetites of diners and catering to them in the most convenient way.

Fruits and sweetmeats were relished. Consequently a bowl or épergne piled pyramid-fashion with one or the other took the place of a bouquet centerpiece. The word "épergne" is from the French *épargne,* meaning a sparing or saving, which suggests that the épergne served a threefold purpose: it was at once decorative, allowed diners to help themselves freely of its offerings, and so saved the bother of passing them around time after time.

The elaborate silver and porcelain épergnes to be seen on dining tables in the Governor's Palace and the Wythe House, made expressly to hold fruit, nuts, and sweetmeats, are also proof that in colonial days fruit was highly regarded as an edible decoration. Not even the everlastings can match the rich colors that fruit adds to a room in the dull days of the year—say, a handful of crab apples in a salt-glaze dish or a pewter bowl, or smooth bright yellow lemons in a basket. That the eighteenth century appreciated the beauty of fruit as decoration, while they relished it as a dessert, is apparent in Robert Furber's handsome fruit prints, which complement his *Twelve Months of Flowers.*

Both English squires and Virginia plantation owners were as much connoisseurs of fruit as of wine. By wisdom born of experience they knew their fruit as wise gardeners know their flowers, knew just the moment to gather, and after proper keeping just the perfect moment to bite and relish.

Then, as now in Virginia, fruit was never hard to come by the year round. Even in the early days of Jamestown, colonists enjoyed it in abundance, so much so that Robert Beverley, in *The History and Present State of Virginia,* attributed much sickness among tobacco-vessel sailors to their eating too much "green Fruit, and unripe Trash" during the hot weather, so that they "fall into Fluxes, Fevers, and the Belly-Ach." But among plantation owners, Beverley noted "many fanciers of beautiful fruits."

The plantation owners, just like the English squires, were enthusiastic growers of fruit, ornamental trees, and flowers. By 1681, John Rea, who described himself as an English Gentleman, referred in his *Flora, Ceres and Pomona* to the profusion of fruit varieties grown. Aside from commoner sorts, he mentioned twenty sorts of apples, twenty kinds of pears, five varieties of quince, six of apricots, one nectarine, and twenty-four kinds of cherries, forty-four of plums, and thirty-five of peaches, besides miscellaneous almonds, nuts, vines, figs, and three kinds of mulberry—black, white, and red.

The planters of tidewater Virginia, from Governor Berkeley of Jamestown to William Byrd II of Westover, followed the squires in becoming devoted growers of all fruit known to the Temperate Zone. The persimmon and the grape were Virginia natives; the fig and the pomegranate also flourished as well there as in the warm countries of southern Europe. Watermelons and muskmelons were kept a good part of the winter in dark cellars (successful keeping depended upon breaking off the stem and burning the broken end with a red-hot iron). Indeed, the land was so fertile that it was said you could sleep while your fruit grew to its full perfection. Besides such home-grown plenty, semi-tropical fruits—oranges and lemons, limes, and that king of fruits, the pineapple—were available on occasion from the West Indies.

Peter Collinson, in sending the pomegranate to John Bartram, be-

▶

40. A silver épergne laden with fruit in the Wythe House dining room. Pineapple and lemons echo the yellow shade of the curtains, chair seats, and painted back of the corner cupboard; apples add a rosy touch.

sought him not to "use the Pomegranate inhospitably, a stranger that has come so far to pay his respect to thee. Don't turn him adrift in the wide world; but plant it against the south side of thy house, nail it close to the wall. In this manner it thrives wonderfully with us, and flowers beautifully and bears fruit this hot year."

It was sound advice for growing this tree of scarlet blossoms whose fruit, reported John Hill, an English writer, if left ungathered "will burst upon the Tree, and show its crimson Grains with vast Beauty." Such advice was not needed in the Tidewater, where the highly ornamental pomegranate was already a part of the landscape. Mark Catesby recorded in his *Natural History* seeing it growing "in great perfection in the Gardens of the Hon. William Byrd, Esq; in the freshes of James river." And there is a note in Byrd's own diary for September 20, 1711, of four pomegranates grown at Westover and sent to the governor in Williamsburg.

So much for a few answers to the questions visitors to Williamsburg ask about the flower and fruit arrangements. The questions, and they are asked by the young and the old, tell plainly that people—wherever they come from, whatever their backgrounds—have the same curiosity about all growing green things as their forebears had more than two hundred years ago. And I like to know that some of that curiosity may be heightened further by what Colonial Williamsburg has to show.

APPENDIX

Plant Material List

A representative list of trees, shrubs, flowers, vines, and herbs that might have been found in the gardens of eighteenth-century Williamsburg or in the surrounding woods and fields.

Absinthe, *Artemisia absinthium*
Acer
  negundo, box elder
  rubrum, red maple
  saccharinum, silver maple
  saccharum, sugar maple
  platanoides, yellow or Norway maple
Achillea
  millefolium, yarrow
  ptarmica, sneezewort yarrow
Aconitum napellus, monkshood
Aesculus
  flava, sweet buckeye
  hippocastanum, horse chestnut
  parviflora, bottle brush buckeye
  pavia, red buckeye
Ageratum, *Ageratum conyzoides*
Agrostis nebulosa, cloud grass
Ajuga (carpet bugle), *Ajuga reptans*
Allium
  ampeloprasum, Yorktown onion
  porrum, leek
  sativum, garlic
  schoenoprasum, chive
Allspice, Carolina, *Calycanthus floridus*
Almond, *Prunus communis*
Althaea rosea, hollyhock
Althaea (rose of Sharon), *Hibiscus syriacus*

Alyssum
  golden tuft, *Alyssum saxatile*
  sweet, *Lobularia maritima*
Amaranth, globe, *Gomphrena globosa*
Amaranthus caudatus, love lies bleeding
Amelanchier canadensis, shadblow
Ammophila breviligulata, beachgrass
Amsonia, *Amsonia tabernaemontana*
Anaphalis margaritacea, pearly everlasting
Andropogon virginicus, broomsedge grass
Anemone, poppy, *Anemone coronaria*
Anethum graveolens, dill
Angelica, *Angelica archangelica*
Anise, *Pimpinella anisum*
Anisostichus capreolata, crossvine
Anthemis
  nobilis, chamomile
  tinctoria, golden chamomile
Anthriscus cerefolium, chervil
Antirrhinum majus, snapdragon
Apple, *Malus pumila*
  southern crab-apple, *M. angustifolia*
  wild sweet crab-apple, *M. coronaria*
Apricot, *Prunus armeniaca*
Aquilegia canadensis, columbine
Arachis hypogaea, peanut

Aralia spinosa, devil's walking stick
Arborvitae, eastern, *Thuja occidentalis*
Argemone, *Argemone grandiflora*
Armeria. *See* Sea lavender
Armoracia rusticana, horseradish
Arrow-wood, *Viburnum dentatum*
Artemisia
    abrotanum, Southernwood
    absinthium, absinthe
    dracunculus, tarragon
    pontica, Roman wormwood
    vulgaris, mugwort
Arundinaria tecta, switchcane
    (dwarf bamboo)
Asclepias
    purpurascens, milkweed
    tuberosa, butterfly weed
Ash, American mountain. *See*
    Mountain ash, American
Ash, white, *Fraxinus americana*
Asimina triloba, pawpaw
Asphodeline lutea, Jacob's rod
Aster (many species)
Aster, China, *Callistephus chinensis*
Atamasco lily, *Zephyranthes atamasco*
Avena sativa, oat
Azalea
    coast, *Rhododendron atlanticum*
    flame, *R. calendulaceum*
    indica, *R. indicum*
    pinxter bloom, *R. nudiflorum*
    swamp white, *R. viscosum*

Baby's breath, *Gypsophila paniculata*
Baccharis halimifolia, saltbush
Baldcypress, *Taxodium distichum*
Balloon flower, *Platycodon grandiflorus*
Balm (lemon balm), *Melissa officinalis*
Baptisia australis, false indigo
Barley, *Hordeum vulgare*
Basil, sweet, *Ocimum basilicum*
Bay, red, *Persea borbonia*
Bayberry, southern. *See* Wax Myrtle

Beard tongue, *Penstemon hirsutus*
Beautyberry, American, *Callicarpa americana*
Bedstraw, *Galium verum*
Bee balm
    Aswego Tea, *Monarda didyma*
    wild bergamot, *M. fistulosa*
Beech, American, *Fagus grandifolia*
Bellflower, peach-leaved, *Campanula persicifolia*
Bellis perennis, English daisy
Bells of Ireland, *Moluccella laevis*
Bergamot. *See* Bee balm
Betula nigra, river birch
Birch, river, *Betula nigra*
Bitternut, *Carya cordiformis*
Bittersweet, *Celastrus scandens*
Black-eyed Susan, *Rudbeckia hirta*
Blazing star, *Liatris elegans*
Bluebell, Spanish, *Scilla hispanica*
Boneset, *Eupatorium perfoliatum*
Borage, *Borago officinalis*
Bouncing Bet, *Saponaria officinalis*
Box
    common, *Buxus sempervirens*
    dwarf, *B. sempervirens suffruticosa*
Broussonetia papyrifera, paper mulberry
Buckeye
    bottle brush, *Aesculus parviflora*
    red, *A. pavia*
    sweet, *A. flava*
Buckthorn
    Carolina, *Rhamnus caroliniana*
    southern, *Bumelia lycioides*
Burnet, *Sanguisorba minor*
Bursting heart (strawberrybush), *Euonymus americanus*
Butcher's broom, *Ruscus aculeatus*
Butterfly weed, *Asclepias tuberosa*
Butternut, *Juglans cinerea*
Button bush, *Cephalanthus occidentalis*
Buxus
    sempervirens, common box
    s. suffruticosa, dwarf box

Calendula, *Calendula officinalis*
Callicarpa americana, American
  beautyberry
Callistephus chinensis, China aster
Caltha palistris, marsh marigold
Calycanthus floridus, sweet shrub
Camassia scilloides, wild hyacinth
Camellia, *Camellia japonica*
Chamomile, *Anthemis nobilis*
  golden, *A. tinctoria*
Campanula
  medium, Canterbury bells
  persicifolia, peach-leaved
    bellflower
  pyramidalis, chimney flower
Campion
  Maltese Cross, *Lychnis chalcedonica*
  rose, *L. coronaria*
Campsis radicans, trumpet creeper
Candytuft, *Iberis sempervirens*
Canterbury bells, *Campanula medium*
Caraway, *Carum carvi*
Cardinal flower. *See* Lobelia, red
Carnation, *Dianthus caryophyllus*
Carpinus caroliniana, American
  hornbeam
Carum carvi, caraway
Carya
  cordiformis, bitternut
  illinoensis, pecan
  laciniosa, shellbark hickory
  ovata, shagbark hickory
  tomentosa, mockernut
Castanea dentata, American chestnut
Catalpa, southern, *Catalpa*
  bignonioides
Catananche caerulea, Cupid's dart
Catnip, *Nepeta cataria*
Cattail, *Typha angustifolia*
Ceanothus americanus, New Jersey tea
Cedar
  Atlantic white, *Chamaecyparis*
    thyoides
  of Lebanon, *Cedrus libani*
  eastern red, *Juniperus virginiana*
Celastrus scandens, bittersweet
Celosia

  argentea cristata, cockscomb
  plumosa, prince's plume
Celtis
  laevigata, sugarberry
  occidentalis, hackberry
Centaurea
  cyanus, cornflower
  gymnocarpa, dusty miller
  moschata, sweet sultan
Centranthus
  ruber, Jupiter's beard
  ruber albus, white Jupiter's beard
Cephalanthus occidentalis, button bush
Cercis canadensis, redbud
Chaenomeles lagenaria, flowering
  quince
Chamaecyparis thyoides, Atlantic white
  cedar
Chaste tree (vitex), *Vitex agnus-castus*
  cutleaf, *V. negundoincisa*
Cheiranthus cheiri, wallflower
Chelone glabra, turtlehead
Cherry
  black, *Prunus serotina*
  sour, *P. cerasus*
  sweet, *P. avium*
  Cornelian, *Cornus mas*
Chervil *Anthriscus cerefolium*
Chestnut, American, *Castanea*
  dentata
Chimney bellflower, *Campanula*
  pyramidalis
Chimonanthus praecox, wintersweet
China aster, *Callistephus chinensis*
Chinaberry, *Melia azedarach*
Chinese lantern, *Physalis alkekengi*
Chionanthus virginicus, fringe tree
Chive, *Allium schoenoprasum*
Chokeberry
  black, *Sorbus melanocarpa*
  red, *arbutifolia*
Chrysanthemum
  balsamita, costmary
  leucanthemum, common daisy
    (ox-eye)
  parthenium, feverfew
Cladrastis lutea, yellowwood

Claytonia virginica, spring beauty
Clematis (virgin's bower), *Clematis*
   virginiana
Cleome spinosa, spiderflower
Clethra alnifolia, sweet pepper bush
Clover, sweet, *Melilotus alba*
Cockscomb, *Celosia argentea cristata*
Coffee tree, Kentucky, *Gymnocladus*
   dioica
Colchicum, *Colchicum autumnale*
Columbine, *Aquilegia canadensis*
Comptonia peregrina, sweet fern
Convallaria majalis, lily of the valley
Coreopsis, *Coreopsis lanceolata*
Coriander, *Coriandrum sativum*
Corn, *Zea mays*
Cornflower, *Centaurea cyanus*
Cornus
   amomum, silky dogwood
   florida, flowering dogwood
   florida rubra, pink flowering
      dogwood
   mas, Cornelian cherry
   stolonifera, red osier dogwood
Costmary, *Chrysanthemum balsamita*
Cotinus coggygria, smokebush
Cotton, *Gossypium barbadense*
Cottonwood, *Populus deltoides*
Crab-apple, *Malus angustifolia*
   wild sweet, *M. coronaria*
Cranberry, highbush, *Viburnum*
   trilobum
Crape myrtle, *Lagerstroemia indica*
Crataegus
   monogyna, English hawthorn
   phaenopyrum, Washington Thorn
Crocus
   fall, *Crocus kotschyanus*
   spring, *C. vernus*
   See also Colchicum
Crossvine, *Anisostichus capreolata*
Crotalaria, *Crotalaria sagittalis*
Crown imperial, *Fritillaria imperialis*
Cucumber tree, *Magnolia acuminata*
Cupid's dart, *Catananche caerulea*
Currant, red, *Ribes sativum*
Cut-and-come-again. *See Helianthus*

Cydonia oblonga, fruiting quince
Cyrilla, swamp (titi), *Cyrilla racemiflora*
Cytisus scoparius, Scotch broom

Daffodil
   common, *Narcissus pseudo-narcissus*
   double white, *N. poeticus plenus*
Dahoon, *Ilex cassine*
Daisy
   common (ox-eye), *Chrysanthemum*
      leucanthemum
   English, *Bellis perennis*
Dame's rocket, *Hesperis matronalis*
Danae racemosa, Alexandrian (poet's)
   laurel
Dangleberry, *Gaylussacia frondosa*
Daucus carota, Queen Anne's lace
Day lily
   lemon, *Hemerocallis flava*
   Tawny, *H. fulva*
Decumaria, *Decumaria barbara*
Deerberry, *Vaccinium stamineum*
Delphinium ajacis, rocket larkspur
Devil's walking stick, *Aralia spinosa*
Devilwood, *Osmanthus americanus*
Dianthus
   barbatus, sweet William
   caryophyllus, carnation
   chinensis, Chinese pink
   plumarius, grass pink
Dictamnus albus, dittany
Digitalis purpurea, foxglove
Dill, *Anethum graveolens*
Diospyros virginiana, persimmon
Dirca palustris, leatherwood
Dittany, *Dictamnus albus*
Dock, *Rumex patientia*
Dogwood
   flowering, *Cornus florida*
   pink flowering, *C. florida rubra*
   red osier, *C. stolonifera*
   silky, *C. amomum*
Doronicum plantagineum, leopard
   bane
Dragonhead, false, *Physostegia*
   virginiana

Dusty miller, *Centaurea gymnocarpa*

Elaeagnus angustifolia, Russian olive
Elder
    American, *Sambucus canadensis*
    box, *Acer negundo*
Elm
    American, *Ulmus americana*
    slippery, *U. rubra*
    winged, *U. alata*
Erianthus ravennae, plume grass
Erigeron canadensis, horseweed
Euonymus americanus, bursting heart
Eupatorium
    coelestinum, mist flower
    perfoliatum, boneset
    purpureum, Joe-pye weed
Euphorbia corollata, flowering spurge
Everlasting, pearly, *Anaphalis mar-*
    garitacea

Fagus grandifolia, American beech
Fennel, *Foeniculum vulgare*
Fennel flower, *Nigella damascena*
Fern
    cinnamon, *Osmunda cinnamomea*
    royal, *O. regalis*
    sweet, *Comptonia peregrina*
Feverbark, Georgia, *Pinckneya*
    pubens
Feverfew, *Chrysanthemum parthenium*
Fig, *Ficus carica*
Firethorn, scarlet, *Pyracantha*
    coccinea
Foam flower, *Tiarella cordifolia*
Foeniculum vulgare, fennel
Fothergilla, dwarf, *Fothergilla*
    gardeni
Four o'clock, *Mirabilis jalapa*
Foxglove, *Digitalis purpurea*
Fragaria, strawberry, spp.
    F. chiloensis
    F. moschata
    F. vesca
    F. virginiana

Franklinia, *Franklinia alatamaha*
Fraxinus americana, white ash
Fringe tree, *Chionanthus virginicus*
Fritillaria
    imperialis, crown imperial
    meleagris, checkered fritillary

Galanthus nivalis, snowdrop
Galax, *Galax aphylla*
Galium verum, bedstraw
Gardenia, *Gardenia jasminoides*
Garlic, *Allium sativum*
Gaylussacia
    baccata, black huckleberry
    dumosa, bush huckleberry
    frondosa, dangleberry
Gelsemium sempervirens, Carolina
    yellow jessamine
Germander, *Teucrium chamaedrys*
Ginkgo (maidenhair tree), *Ginkgo*
    biloba
Gladiolus, *Gladiolus blandus*
Gleditsia triacanthos, honey locust
Globe amaranth. *See* Amaranth,
    globe
Goldenrain tree, panicled,
    Koelreuteria paniculata
Goldenrod
    Canada, *Solidago altissima*
    fragrant, *S. odora*
    plume, *S. juncea*
    silver, *S. bicolor*
    wreath, *S. caesia*
    wrinkled, *S. rugosa*
Gomphrena globosa, globe
    amaranth
Good King Henry (goosefoot),
    Chenopodium bonus-henricus
Gossypium barbadense, cotton
Grape
    chicken, *Vitis cordifolia*
    fox, *V. labrusca*
    muscadine, *V. rotundifolia*
    summer, *V. aestivalis*
    wine, *V. vinifera*
Grass

beachgrass, *Ammophila breviligulata*
broom-sedge, *Andropogon virginicus*
cloud, *Agrostis nebulosa*
fox-tail, *Setaria magna*
plume, *Erianthus ravennae*
spike, *Uniola latifolia*
Gum
    cotton (tupelo), *Nyssa aquatica*
    sour (black), *N. sylvatica*
    sweet, *Liquidambar styraciflua*
Gymnocladus dioica, Kentucky coffee
    tree
Gypsophilia paniculata, baby's breath

Hackberry, *Celtis occidentalis*
Halesia carolina, Carolina silverbell
Hamemelis virginiana, witch hazel
Haw
    black, *Viburnum prunifolium*
    possum, *Ilex decidua*
Hawthorn
    English, *Crataegus monogyna*
    Washington, *C. phaenopyrum*
Hedera helix, English ivy
Helenium (sneezeweed), *Helenium*
    autumnale
Helianthus
    angustifolius, swamp sunflower
    annuus, common sunflower
        (cut-and-come-again)
    decapetalus, river sunflower
    giganteus, giant sunflower
    tuberosus, Jerusalem artichoke
Helichrysum bractaetum, strawflower
Heliotrope, *Heliotropium*
Helleborus niger, Christmas rose
Hemerocallis
    flava, lemon day lily
    fulva, tawny day lily
Hemlock, eastern, *Tsuga canadensis*
Hesperis matronalis, dame's rocket
Hibiscus
    moscheutos, rose (swamp) mallow
    syriacus, shrub althea
Hickory
    shagbark, *Carya ovata*

shellbark, *C. laciniosa*
Highbush cranberry. *See* Cranberry
Holly
    American, *Ilex opaca*
    dahoon, *I. cassine*
    English, *I. aquifolium*
    myrtle-leaved, *I. myrtifolia*
    yaupon, *I. vomitoria*
Hollyhock, *Althaea rosea*
Honesty, *Lunaria annua*
Honeysuckle
    coral, *Lonicera sempervirens*
    Tatarian, *L. tatarica*
Hoptree, *Ptelea trifoliata*
Hordeum vulgare, barley
Horehound, *Marrubium vulgare*
Hornbeam, American, *Carpinus*
    caroliniana
Horse chestnut, *Aesculus hippo-*
    castanum
Horseradish, *Armoracia rusticana*
Horseweed, *Erigeron canadensis*
Huckleberry
    black, *Gaylussacia baccata*
    bush, *G. dumosa*
Hydrangea
    oakleaf, *Hydrangea quercifolia*
    smooth, *H. arborescens*
Hypericum
    calycinum, St. John's wort
    densiflorum, bushy St. John's wort
Hyssop, *Hyssopus officinalis*

Ilex
    aquifolium, English holly
    cassine, dahoon
    decidua, possum haw
    glabra, inkberry
    myrtifolia, myrtle-leaved holly
    opaca, American holly
    verticillata, winterberry
    vomitoria, yaupon
Indian currant (coralberry),
    Symphoricarpos orbiculatus
Indigo, false, *Baptisia australis*
Inkberry, *Ilex glabra*

Iris
  blue, *Iris pallida*
  German, *I. germanica*
  Siberian, *I. sibirica*
  Spanish, *I. xiphium*
  yellow flag, *I. pseudacorus*
Itea virginiana, sweet spire
Ivy
  Boston, *Ampelopsis tricuspidata*
  English, *Hedera helix*
  Poison, *Rhus radicans*

Jacob's rod, *Asphodeline lutea*
Jamestown or atamasco lily,
   Zephyranthes atamasco
Jasmine, *Jasminum officinale*
Jerusalem artichoke, *Helianthus
   tuberosus*
Jessamine, Carolina yellow,
   Gelsemium sempervirens
Joe-pye-weed,*Eupatorium purpureum*
Jonquil, *Narcissus jonquilla*
  Campernelle, *N. odorus*
Judas tree. *See* redbud
Juglans
  cinerea, butternut
  nigra, black walnut
  regia, English walnut
Juniperus virginiana, red cedar
Jupiter's beard, *Centranthus ruber*
  white, *C. ruber albus*

Kalmia latifolia, mountain laurel
Koelreuteria paniculata, panicled goldenrain tree

Laburnum, *Laburnum anagyroides*
Lagerstroemia indica, crape myrtle
Lantana, *Lantana camara*
Larkspur, rocket, *Dephinium ajacis*
Lathyrus odoratus, sweet pea
Laurel
  Alexandrian (poet's), *Danae race-
   mosa*

cherry, *Prunus caroliniana*
  English, *P. laurocerasus*
Laurustinus, *Viburnum tinus*
Lavender, *Lavandula angustifolius*
  cotton, cypress, *Santolina chamae-
   cyparissus*
  cotton, green, *S. virens*
Leek, *Allium porrum*
Leatherwood, *Dirca palustris*
Leopard bane, *Doronicum plantagin-
  eum*
Leucothoë
  coast, *Leucothoë axillaris*
  drooping *L. fontanesiana*
Levisticum officinale, lovage
Liatris elegans, blazing star
Ligustrum vulgare, privet
Lilac
  common, *Syringa vulgaris*
  Persian, *S. persica*
  Rouen, *S. chinensis*
Lily
  Guernsey, *Nerine sarniensis*
  Jamestown or atamasco, *Zephyran-
   thes atamasco*
  Madonna, *Lilium candidum*
  meadow, *L. canadense*
  scarlet, *L. philadelphicum*
  Turk's cap, *L. superbum*
  See also Hemerocallis
Lily of the valley, *Convallaria majalis*
Linden
  American, *Tilia americana*
  small-leaved, *T. cordata*
Lindera benzoin, spice bush
Liquidambar styraciflua, sweet gum
Liriodendron tulipifera, tulip tree
Lobelia
  blue, *Lobelia siphilitica*
  red, *L. cardinalis*
Lobularia maritima, sweet alyssum
Locust
  black, *Robinia pseudoacacia*
  honey, *Gleditsia triacanthos*
  roseacacia, *Robinia hispida*
Lonicera
  sempervirens, coral honeysuckle

Nasturtium, *Tropaeolum majus*
Nectarine, *Prunus persica nectarina*
Nepeta cataria catnip
Nerine sarniensis, Guernsey lily
Nerium oleander, oleander
New Jersey tea, *Ceanothus americanus*
Nicotiana tabacum, white burley tobacco
Nigella N. damascena, fennel flower
Nyssa
    aquatica, cotton (tupelo) gum
    sylvatica, sour (black) gum

Oak
    basket, *Quercus michauxii*
    black, *Q. velutina*
    black jack, *Q. marilandica*
    chestnut, *Q. prinus*
    Darlington, *Q. hemisphaerica*
    English, *Q. robur*
    live, *Q. virginiana*
    red, *Q. rubra*
    scarlet, *Q. coccinea*
    shingle, *Q. imbricaria*
    southern red, *Q. falcata*
    swamp white, *Q. bicolor*
    water, *Q. nigra*
    white, *Q. alba*
    willow, *Q. phellos*
Oat, *Avena sativa*
Ocimum basilicum, sweet basil
Oenothera biennis, evening primrose
Oleander, *Nerium oleander*
Olive, Russian, *Elaeagnus angustifolia*
Oregano, Origanum *O. mexicana*
Ornithogalum umbellatum, Star-of-Bethlehem
Osage orange, *Maclura pomifera*
Osmanthus americanus, devilwood
Osmunda
    cinnamomea, cinnamon fern
    regalis, royal fern
Oxydendrum arboreum, sorrel tree

Paeonia officinalis, peony

Pagoda tree (scholar tree), Japanese, *Sophora japonica*
Pansy, *Viola tricolor hortensis*
Papaver
    orientale, Oriental poppy
    rhoeas, corn poppy
    somniferum, carnation-flowered poppy
Parsley, *Petroselinum crispum*
Parthenocissus quinquefolia, Virginia creeper
Partridgeberry, *Mitchella repens*
Passion flower, wild (maypop), *Passiflora incarnata*
Pawpaw, *Asimina tribola*
Peach, *Prunus persica*
    flowering, *P. persica var.*
Peanut, *Arachis hypogaea*
Pear, *Pyrus communis*
Pecan, *Carya illinoensis*
Pennyroyal, *Mentha pulegium*
Penstemon hirsutus, beard tongue
Peony, *Paeonia officinalis*
Pepper bush, sweet, *Clethra alnifolia*
Peppermint, *Mentha piperita*
Periwinkle, *Vinca major*
    common, *V. minor*
Persimmon, *Diospyros virginiana*
Persea borbonia, red bay
Petroselinum crispum, parsley
Philadelphus coronarius, mock orange
Phlox
    summer, *Phlox paniculata*
    sweet William, *P. divaricata*
Phoradendron serotinum, mistletoe
Physalis alkekengi, Chinese lantern
Physostegia virginiana, false dragonhead
Picea abies, Norway spruce
Pickerel weed, *Pontederia cordata*
Pimpinella anisum, anise
Pine
    cluster, *Pinus pinaster*
    loblolly, *P. taeda*
    shortleaf, *P. echinata*
    Virginia, *P. virginiana*
    white, *P. strobus*

Pink
   Chinese, *Dianthus chinensis*
   grass, *D. plumarius*
Platanus occidentalis, sycamore
Platycodon grandiflorum, balloon
   flower
Plum
   beach, *Prunus maritima*
   Chickasaw, *P. angustifolia*
   common, *P. domestica*
Poker, red hot, *Kniphofia uvaria*
Polianthes tuberosa, tuberose
Pomegranate, *Punica granatum*
Pontederia cordata, pickerel weed
Poplar, Lombardy, *Populus nigra*
   italica
Poppy
   carnation-flowered, *Papaver*
     somniferum
   corn, *P. rhoeas*
   Oriental, *P. orientale*
Populus
   deltoides, cottonwood
   nigra italica, Lombardy poplar
Primrose
   evening, *Oenothera biennis*
   polyantha, *Primula polyantha*
Privet, *Ligustrum vulgare*
Prince's plume, *Celosia plumosa*
Prunus
   angustifolia, Chickasaw plum
   armeniaca, apricot
   avium, sweet cherry
   cerasus, sour cherry
   communis, almond
   domestica, plum
   maritima, beach plum
   persica, peach
   persica nectarina, nectarine
   serotina, black cherry
Ptelea trifoliata, hoptree
Punica granatum, pomegranate
Pussy willow, *Salix discolor*
Pyracantha coccinea, scarlet firethorn
Pyrus communis, pear

Queen Anne's lace, *Daucus carota*
Quercus
   alba, white oak
   bicolor, swamp white oak
   coccinea, scarlet oak
   falcata, southern red oak
   hemisphaerica, Darlington
   imbricaria, shingle
   marilandica, black jack oak
   michauxii, basket oak
   nigra, water oak
   phellos, willow oak
   prinus, chestnut oak
   robus, English oak
   rubra, red oak
   velutina, black oak
   virginiana, live oak
Quince
   flowering, *Chaenomeles lagenaria*
   fruiting, *Cydonia oblonga*

Ragwort, golden, *Senecio aureus*
Raspberry
   blackcap, *Rubus occidentalis*
   flowering (fragrant thimble-
     berry), *R. odoratus*
   red, *R. idaeus*
Redbud, *Cercis canadensis*
Rhamnus caroliniana, Carolina
   buckthorn
Rhododendron
   atlanticum, coast azalea
   calendulaceum, flame azalea
   indicum, indica azalea
   nudiflorum, pinxter bloom azalea
   viscosum, swamp white azalea
Rhus
   aromatica, fragrant sumac
   copallina, shining sumac
   glabra, smooth sumac
   radicans, poison ivy
   typhina, staghorn sumac
Ribes sativum, red currant
Robinia
   hispida, roseacacia locust
   pseudoacacia, black locust

Rose
  Burnett (Scotch), *Rosa spinosissima*
  cabbage, *R. centifolia*
  Cherokee, *R. laevigata*
  Christmas, *Helleborus niger*
  damask, *Rosa damascena*
  French, *R. gallica*
  moss, *R. centifolia muscosa*
  rosamundi, *R. gallica versicolor*
  swamp, *R. palustris*
  sweetbrier, *R. eglanteria*
  Virginia, *R. virginiana*
  York and Lancaster, R. *damascena
    versicolor*
Rosemary, *Rosmarinus officinalis*
Rubus
  idaeus, European raspberry
  occidentalis, blackcap raspberry
  odoratus, flowering raspberry
    (fragrant thimbleberry)
Rudbeckia hirta, black-eyed Susan
Rue, *Ruta graveolens*
Rumex
  patientia, dock
  scutatus, French sorrel
Ruscus aculeatus, butcher's broom
Ruta graveolens, rue

Sage
  clary, *Salvia sclarea*
  garden, *S. officinalis*
  scarlet, *S. splendens*
St. John's wort, *Hypericum calycinum*
  bushy, *H. densiflorum*
Salix
  babylonica, weeping willow
  discolor, pussy willow
Saltbush, *Baccharis halimifolia*
Salvia
  officinalis, garden sage
  sclarea, clary sage
  splendens, scarlet sage
Sambucus canadensis, American elder
Sanguisorba minor, burnet
Santolina chamaecyparissus, lavender
  cotton

S. virens, green lavender cotton
Saponaria officinalis, bouncing Bet
Sassafras, *Sassafras albidum*
Savory
  summer, *Satureja hortensis*
  winter, *S. montana*
Scabiosa atropurpurea, mourning
  bride
Scilla
  hispanica, Spanish bluebell
  siberica, Siberian squill
Scotch broom, *Cytisus scoparius*
Sea lavender (statice), *Limonium
  latifolium*
Senecio aureus, golden ragwort
Setaria magna, foxtail grass
Shadblow, *Amelanchier canadensis*
Silverbell, Carolina, *Halesia carolina*
Skunk cabbage, *symplocarpus foetidus*
Smilax (laurel-leaf greenbrier),
  Smilax laurifolia
Smokebush, *Cotinus coggygria*
Snapdragon, *Antirrhinum majus*
Sneezeweed, *Helenium autumnale*
Snowball bush, *Viburnum opulus
  roseum*
Snowbell, *Styrax americana*
Snowdrop, *Galanthus nivalis*
Solidago
  altissima, Canada goldenrod
  bicolor, silver goldenrod
  caesia, wreath goldenrod
  juncea, plume goldenrod
  odora, fragrant goldenrod
  rugosa, wrinkled goldenrod
Sophora japonica, Japanese pagoda
  (or scholar) tree
Sorbus americana, American
  mountain ash
  arbutifolia, red chokeberry
  melanocarpa, black chokeberry
Sorrel, French, *Rumex scutatus*
Sorrel tree, *Oxydendrum arboreum*
Southernwood, *Artemisia abrotanum*
Spearmint, *Mentha spicata*
Speedwell. *See Veronica*
Spice bush, *Lindera benzoin*

Spider flower, *Cleome spinosa*
Spiderlily, *Lycoris radiata*
Spiderwort, *Tradescantia
    virginiana*
Spire, sweet, *Itea virginiana*
Spirea, white, *Spirea tomentosa alba*
Spring beauty, *Claytonia virginica*
Spruce, Norway, *Picea abies*
Spurge, flowering, *Euphorbia
    corollata*
Squill. *See Scilla*
Stachys
    ciliata, betony
    lanata, wooly betony (lamb's ears)
Star-of-Bethlehem, *Ornithogalum
    umbellatum*
    drooping, *O. nutans*
Statice. *See* Sea lavender
Sternbergia, *Sternbergia lutea*
Stewartia, *Stewartia malachodendron*
    mountain, *S. ovata*
Stock, *Matthiola incana*
Stokesia, *Stokesia laevis*
Strawberry. *See Fragaria*
Strawberrybush (bursting heart),
    Euonymus americanus
Strawflower, *Helichrysum bracteatum*
Styrax americana, American snowbell
Sugarberry, *Celtis laevigata*
Sumac
    fragrant, *Rhus aromatica*
    shining, *R. copallina*
    smooth, *R. glabra*
    staghorn, *R. typhina*
Sunflower
    common, *Helianthus annuus*
    giant, *H. giganteus*
    river, *H. decapetalus*
    swamp, *H. angustifolius*
Sweet pea, *Lathyrus odoratus*
Sweet shrub (Carolina allspice),
    Calycanthus floridus
Sweet sultan, *Centaurea moschata*
Sweet William, *Dianthus barbatus*
Switchcane (dwarf bamboo),
    Arundinaria tecta
Sycamore (American plane),

Platanus occidentalis
Symphoricarpos orbiculatus, Indian
    currant (coralberry)
Symplocarpus foetidus, skunk cabbage
Syringa
    chinensis, Rouen lilac
    persica, Persian lilac
    vulgaris, lilac

Tagetes
    erecta, Aztec marigold
    patula, French marigold
Tanacetum vulgare, tansy
Tansy, *Tanacetum vulgare*
Tarragon, *Artemisia dracunculus*
Taxodium distichum, baldcypress
Taxus baccata, English yew
Tea shrub, *Camellia sinensis*
Teucrium chamaedrys, germander
Thalictrum minus, meadow rue
Thermopsis, *Thermopsis caroliniana*
    soft, *T. mollis*
Thimbleberry, fragrant (flowering
    raspberry), *Rubus odoratus*
Thuja occidentalis, eastern arborvitae
Thyme, *Thymus vulgaris*
Titi. *See* Cyrilla, swamp
Tiarella cordifolia, foam flower
Tilia
    americana, American linden
    cordata, small-leaved linden
Tobacco, white burley, *Nicotiana
    tabacum*
Tradescantia virginiana, spiderwort
Triticum aestivum, wheat
Tropaeolum majus, nasturtium
Trumpet creeper, *Campsis radicans*
Tsuga canadensis, eastern hemlock
Tuberose, *Polianthes tuberosa*
Tulip, in variety, *Tulipa spp.*
Tulip tree, *Liriodendron tulipifera*
Tupelo. *See* Gum
Turtlehead, *Chelone glabra*
Typha angustifolia, cattail

Ulmus
  alata, winged elm
  americana, American elm
  rubra, American elm
Umbrella magnolia, *Magnolia
    tripetala*
Uniola latifolia, spike grass

Vaccinium stamineum, deerberry
Valerian, *Valeriana officinalis. See also*
    Jupiter's beard
Veronica
  arvensis, common speedwell
  longifolia subsessilis, clump
    speedwell
  officinalis, speedwell
  serpyllifolia, thymeleaf speedwell
  spicata, spike speedwell
Viburnum
  acerifolium, mapleleaf viburnum
  cassinoides, witherod
  dentatum, arrow-wood
  lantana, wayfaring tree
  lentago, nannyberry
  opulus roseum, snowball bush
  prunifolium, black haw
  tinus, laurustinus
  tribolum, highbush cranberry
Vinca
  major, periwinkle
  minor, common periwinkle
Viola tricolor hortensis, pansy
Violet, sweet, *Viola odorata*
Virginia creeper, *Parthenocissus
    quinquefolia*
Virgin's bower (clematis), *Clematis
    virginiana*
Vitex (chaste tree), *Vitex agnus-castus*
Vitis

aestivalis, summer grape
cordifolia, frost grape
labrusca, fox grape
rotundifolia, muscadine grape
vinifera, wine grape
Wallflower, *Cheiranthus cheiri*
Walnut
  black, *Juglans nigra*
  English, *J. regia*
Wax myrtle, *Myrica cerifera*
Wayfaring tree, *Viburnum lantana*
Wheat, *Triticum aestivum*
Willow
  pussy, *Salix discolor*
  weeping, *S. babylonica*
Winterberry, *Ilex verticillata*
Wintersweet, *Chimonanthus praecox*
Wisteria, American, *Wisteria fru-
    tescens*
Witch hazel, *Hamamelis virginiana*
Witherod, *Viburnum cassinoides*
Wormwood, Roman, *Artemisia
    pontica*

Yarrow, *Achillea millefolium*
  sneezewort, *A. ptarmica*
Yaupon, *Ilex vomitoria*
Yellowwood, *Cladrastis lutea*
Yew, English, *Taxus baccata*
Yorktown onion, *Allium ampelo-
    prasum*
Yucca
  Adam's needle, *Yucca filamentosa*
  Spanish dagger, *Y. gloriosa*

Zea mays, corn
Zephyranthes atamasco, atamasco or
    Jamestown lily

Bibliography

ALLAN, MEA. *The Tradescants: Their Plants, Gardens and Museum.* London: Joseph, 1964.

AMHERST, ALICIA. *A History of Gardening in England.* 2nd ed. London: Bernard Quaritch, 1896.

ANDREWS, A. W. *The Coming of the Flowers.* London: Williams and Norgate, 1950.

BERRALL, JULIA S. *The Garden: An Illustrated History.* New York: Viking Press, 1966.

——. *A History of Flower Arrangement.* London: Thomas Y. Crowell Co., 1953.

BEVERLEY, ROBERT. *The History and Present State of Virginia.* Edited by Louis B. Wright. Chapel Hill, N. C.: University of North Carolina Press, 1947.

BLUNT, WILFRED. *The Art of Botanical Illustration.* London: Collins, 1950.

BRIDENBAUGH, CARL. *Seat of Empire.* Williamsburg, Va.: Colonial Williamsburg, 1950.

BROTHERSTON, R. P. *The Book of Cut Flowers.* London: T. N. Foulis, 1906.

BUTLER, JUNE RAINSFORD. *Floralia: Garden Paths and By-paths of the Eighteenth Century.* Chapel Hill, N. C.: University of North Carolina Press, 1938.

BYRD, WILLIAM. *William Byrd's Natural History of Virginia.* Translated and edited by Richmond Croom Beatty and William J. Mulloy. Richmond, Va.: Dietz Press, 1950.

COATS, ALICE M. *Flowers and Their Histories.* London: A. & C. Black, 1968.

——. *Garden Shrubs and Their Histories.* London: Studio Vista Ltd., 1964.

——. *The Quest for Plants: A History of the Horticultural Explorers.* London: Studio Vista Ltd., 1969.

COLONIAL WILLIAMSBURG FOUNDATION. *Official Guidebook.* Williamsburg, Va.: Colonial Williamsburg, 1972.

DEWOLF, GORDON P., and FAVRETTI, RUDY F. *Colonial Gardens.* Barre, Mass.: Barre Publishers, 1972.

DREWITT, F. DAWTREY. *The Romance of the Apothecaries' Garden at Chelsea.* 3rd ed. Cambridge: University Press, 1928.

DUTTON, JOAN PARRY. *Enjoying America's Gardens.* New York: Reynal & Co., 1958.

EIFERT, VIRGINIA S. *Tall Trees and Far Horizons: Adventures and Discoveries of Early Botanists in America.* New York: Dodd, Meade & Co., 1965.

123

FISHER, LOUISE B. *An Eighteenth-Century Garland: The Flower and Fruit Arrangements of Colonial Williamsburg.* Williamsburg, Va.: Colonial Williamsburg, 1951.

FRICK, GEORGE FREDERICK, and STEARNS, RAYMOND PHINEAS. *Mark Catesby: The Colonial Audubon.* Urbana, Ill.: University of Illinois Press, 1961.

HADFIELD, MILES. *Gardening in Britain.* London: Hutchison & Co. Ltd., 1960.

——. *Topiary and Ornamental Hedges: Their History and Cultivation.* London: A. & C. Black, 1971.

HARVEY, JOHN. *Early Gardening Catalogues.* London: Phillimore & Co. Ltd., 1972.

HERNDON, MELVIN. *Tobacco in Colonial Virginia, "The Sovereign Remedy."* Jamestown 350th Anniversary Historical Booklets, No. 20. Williamsburg, Va.: Virginia 350th Anniversary Celebration Corporation, 1957.

JONES, HUGH. *The Present State of Virginia.* Edited by Richard L. Morton. Chapel Hill, N. C.: University of North Carolina Press, 1956.

KOCHER, A. LAWRENCE, and DEARSTYNE, HOWARD. *Colonial Williamsburg: Its Buildings and Gardens.* Williamsburg, Va.: Colonial Williamsburg, 1949.

LAW, ERNEST. *A Short History of Hampton Court.* London: George Bell and Sons, 1906.

LEIGHTON, ANN. *Early American Gardens: "For Meate or Medicine."* Boston: Houghton Mifflin Co., 1970.

MARCUS, MARGARET FAIRBANKS. *Period Flower Arrangement.* New York: M. Barrows & Co., Inc., 1952.

SANDS, MILLIE. *The Gardens of Hampton Court: Four Centuries of English History and Gardening.* London: Evans Brothers, 1950.

SWEM, E. G., ed. "Brothers of the Spade: Correspondence of Peter Collinson, of London, and of John Custis, of Williamsburg, Virginia, 1734–1746." American Antiquarian Society, *Proceedings,* LVIII (1948), 17–190.

TAYLOR, NORMAN, ed. *Taylor's Encyclopedia of Gardening.* 4th ed. Boston: Houghton Mifflin Co., 1961.

TAYLOR, RAYMOND L. *Plants of Colonial Days.* Williamsburg, Va.: Colonial Williamsburg, 1952.

TRIGGS, H. INIGO. *Garden Craft in Europe.* London: B. T. Batsford, 1913.

TYLER-WHITTLE, MICHAEL SIDNEY. *The Plant Hunters.* London: Heinemann, 1970.

VIRGINIA WRITERS' PROJECT. *Virginia: A Guide to the Old Dominion.* New York: Oxford University Press, 1940.

WETHERED, H. N. *A Short History of Gardens.* London: Methuen & Co. Ltd., 1933.

Index